Voyage
Le Corbusier

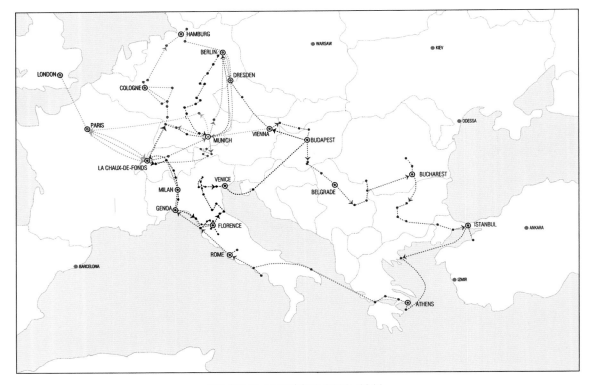

TRAVEL ROUTES 1902–1911

1. La Chaux-de-Fonds—L'École d'art (1902–1907)

2. Italy (September–November 1907)

3. Europe (November 1907–December 1909)

4. Germany (April 1910–May 1911)

5. The East (May–November 1911)

Voyage
Le Corbusier

DRAWING ON THE ROAD

Jacob Brillhart

W. W. Norton & Company

New York • London

Copyright © 2016 by Jacob Brillhart

For information about permission to reproduce selections from this book, write to Permissions, W. W. Norton & Company, Inc., 500 Fifth Avenue, New York, NY 10110

For information about special discounts for bulk purchases, please contact W. W. Norton Special Sales at specialsales@wwnorton.com or 800-233-4830

Manufacturing by Asia Pacific Offset
Book design by Jonathan D. Lippincott
Production manager: Christine Critelli

Library of Congress Cataloging-in-Publication Data
Brillhart, Jacob.
    Voyage Le Corbusier : drawing on the road / Jacob Brillhart ; Foreword by Jean-Louis Cohen. — First Edition.
        pages   cm
    Includes bibliographical references and index.
    ISBN 978-0-393-73356-3 (hardcover)
1. Le Corbusier, 1887–1965—Notebooks, sketchbooks, etc. 2. Le Corbusier, 1887–1965—Travel. 3. Architectural drawing. I. Cohen, Jean-Louis, writer of foreword. II. Le Corbusier, 1887–1965. Drawings. Selections. III. Title.
    NA2707.L4B75 2016
    720.22·22—dc23
                                                                    2015026038

ISBN: 978-0-393-73356-3

W. W. Norton & Company, Inc.
www.wwnorton.com
W. W. Norton & Company, Castle House, 75/76 Wells Street, London W1T 3QT

0 9 8 7 6 5 4 3 2 1

Contents

Foreword: The Wandering Swiss

Jean-Louis Cohen

In his best-selling manifesto *Vers une architecture* (*Toward an Architecture*), a book released in 1923 and soon after that to be translated into German, English, Japanese, and Spanish, Le Corbusier devoted three chapters to "eyes that do not see." The objects his contemporaries ignored were exclusively technical—airplanes, automobiles, ocean liners—but were set against ancient monuments such as the Parthenon, thus revealing, beneath the celebration of modern technology, the passion the young architect entertained for Europe's past. Another expression of this duality can be found in a map documenting his "useful travel" through the Old World, published in 1925 in *The Decorative Art of Today.* Dots corresponding to the cities he visited mark in each case the presence of "culture," "folklore," or "industry," or the coincidence of more than one of these domains.

For seven years, between his initial trip to Tuscany of 1907 and his return to his hometown of La Chaux-de-Fonds, where he established his practice in 1912, Charles-Édouard Jeanneret—the name he carried until 1920—not only discovered specific places and their dominant character but also encountered the profound divides that characterized Europe on the eve of the First World War. Alert to industrial developments in Germany, he also perceived the rising imperialism of the Second Reich, which he would criticize vehemently during the war. Inspired by his contact with the writer William Ritter, he discovered the latent conflict between Germanic and Mediterranean cultures, and the tensions between the Slavs and the Turks.

Avid to record his intense perceptions, Jeanneret used all the media he could handle to convey his travel experience. He learned to write thanks to the frequent letters sent to Ritter, to his parents, and to his first mentor, Charles L'Eplattenier. He used photography extensively; he would never regain his passion for this practice except briefly in the mid-1930s. He also incorporated reminiscences in the buildings he designed in his hometown, as if they were three-dimensional autobiographical statements, in which architectonic details from Italy, Turkey, and Germany were collaged. But the most compelling vehicle for the recording of landscapes, buildings, and their details were the sketches that he systematically drew on the road. Made on loose sheets or in albums of various sizes, including pocket sketchbooks, which he continued to use until the 1960s, using pencil, ink, or watercolors, the drawings were instrumental in helping him secure his first jobs in the offices of Auguste Perret and Peter Behrens. Le Corbusier never systematically published these sketches during his lifetime, although he reproduced dozens of them in the first volume of his *Complete Work*, printed in 1930, and in several post–World War II books. Although some of them have been lost (such as his Paris sketchbooks of the years 1912 to 1917, which may possibly resurface one day), they are for the most part accessible to the scholarly public, thanks to systematic collections published since the early 1980s.

Jacob Brillhart has undertaken a sort of metavoyage among the hundreds of drawings documenting Jeanneret's early travel, in which the curiosity of the young architect appears in its astonishing extension, from the silhouettes of cities such as Istanbul or Rome to decorative details, and from the key monuments of antiquity or the Renaissance to vernacular farms and barns. Jeanneret is by no mean the first architect to have graphically recorded his experience: he echoes the sketches left by Villard de Honnecourt in the thirteenth century, and by many others interested sometimes in the very same sites and buildings; Jeanneret echoes and expands their notations. His prolific graphic oeuvre conveys the amazing observation skills and the relentless imagination of a young artist, all too often forgotten, as the image he would later sculpt for himself would be that of the prophet of the machine age. Yet the public statements of his mature age will never repress the more secret labor of the wandering poet.

Acknowledgments

I would like to express my gratitude to those who helped make this book possible. I am forever indebted to Andrew McNair, Errol Barron, my mother, and my sister for sharing their love of drawing, and to Le Corbusier scholars who came before me—Mary Patricia May Sekler, Stanislaus Von Moos, Geoffrey Baker, Giuliano Gresleri, Jean-Louis Cohen, and H. Allen Brooks—whose research was invaluable in framing my own analyses. Special thanks go to the Fondation Le Corbusier for giving me access to these drawings and to Meghan Campbell, Anna Baez, and Andrew Aquart in my own office for their assistance with supporting graphics. I thank my editor, Nancy Green, for giving me the opportunity to write this and for her continued patience and editorial comments along the way. Finally, very special thanks go to my wife, Melissa Brillhart, for her unwavering love, hard work, and support.

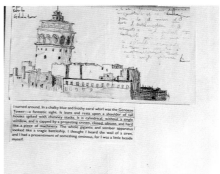

I turned around. In a chalky blue and frothy coral whirl was the Genoese Tower—a fantastic sight. It leans and rests upon a shoulder of tall houses spiked with chimney stacks. It is cylindrical, without a single window, and is capped by a projecting crown, closed, obtuse, and hard like a piece of machinery. The whole gigantic and somber apparatus looked like a tragic battleship. I thought I heard the wail of a siren, and I had a presentiment of something ominous, for I was a little beside myself.

Sketch of Pera Tower (Istanbul, 2010) by Jacob Brillhart, with Jeanneret's 1911 sketch of the same location pasted into my own sketchbook.

Preface

Assembled in this book are more than 140 travel drawings, sketches, and watercolors by Le Corbusier. Born Charles-Édouard Jeanneret on October 6, 1887, he was thirty-three years old and a practicing architect in Paris when he adopted the pseudonym Le Corbusier. (I refer to him as Jeanneret when discussing his life up to 1920 and as Le Corbusier after 1920.) These graphic records of his youthful tours of Europe and the Mediterranean show time and again his gigantic appetite for travel and visual exploration; looking and drawing to see and to understand in order to know.

I became familiar with these drawings during a series of European road trips after graduate school, when I set out to rediscover the forgotten practice of drawing on the road. I used Jeanneret's sketchbooks as my travel guides, retracing his steps through Europe and the East during 1907–1911, observing, photographing, and making drawings from actual places Jeanneret stood some ninety years earlier. Looking at his drawings taught me that we can do something that the computer will never be able to do—draw what we see. In addition, I began to understand how he used drawing as a method of research and how his recording process evolved over time, from his early years of beautifully detailed watercolor drawings to analytical sketches and shorthand visual note taking. I found both his commitment to—and also what he learned through the continued practice of—drawing to be particularly insightful in today's digital world, especially as I watched my architecture students become less and less adept at drawing and thoughtful observation over the course of ten years of teaching. These experiences served as the impetus for this publication.

No single book provides a succinct compendium of Jeanneret's inspiring early watercolor drawings. In sifting through hundreds of files at the Fondation Le Corbusier, I found a large number of works that had never been published. Most of the travel drawings that have been reproduced did not appear in color or in a format large enough to convey the vibrancy and feeling of the work.

This collection of drawings and paintings is meant to serve as a condensed travel handbook and road map for students, architects, art and architecture enthusiasts, design historians, and travelers who care about Le Corbusier or just about the process of learning through travel drawing. I have organized my selection into five sections, two of which are based on formal drawing tours, the Italy tour and what has become known as the Journey to the East. The other three sections outline significant time periods (including two stints away from home) that were critical in forming Jeanneret's early drawing education. This sequence has been established by many previous scholars and is supported by Jeanneret's sketchbooks and letters. The everyday details and timeline of Jeanneret's travel itineraries are taken from the extensive research of H. Allen Brooks in *Le Corbusier's Formative Years*. Geoffrey Baker's book, *Le Corbusier: The Creative Search,* also provided details of his travels and includes translations of the notes that accompany many of Jeanneret's drawings; Giuliano Gresleri's *Les Voyages d'Allemagne* and *Voyage d'Orient: Carnets* also provide Jeanneret's sketchbook notes from Germany and his travels to the East.

To show how Jeanneret's process evolved over time, the drawings are shown predominantly in chronological order, particularly in the case of the two formal drawing tours, where Jeanneret followed travel itineraries. However, fewer dates are available for the drawings made while he was in secondary school in La Chaux-de-Fonds. In the case of travel where Jeanneret was not on a specific itinerary but rather working and/or visiting abroad, the images are not always chronological; some are grouped in ways to most clearly show the evolution of the drawings in terms of technique, media, and subject matter.

With three exceptions—two postcards from La Chaux-de-Fonds Library and one drawing from the Institut für Geschichte und Theorie der Architektur ETH Zurich—all the drawings here belong to the Fondation Le Corbusier and the identification of each contains description, date, media, dimensions (in centimeters, height by width), credit. Where any of this data is omitted, it could not be ascertained.

The maps of Jeanneret's travels were made by my office, Brillhart Architecture, and were built from dates mined from Brooks's text.

Introduction: Learning to See

Le Corbusier was a deeply radical and progressive architect, a futurist who was equally and fundamentally rooted in history and tradition. He was intensely curious, constantly traveling, drawing, painting, and writing, all in the pursuit of becoming a better designer. As a result, he found intellectual ways to connect his historical foundations with what he learned from his contemporaries. He grew from drawing nature to copying fourteenth-century Italian painting to leading the Purist movement that greatly influenced French painting and architecture in the early 1920s. All the while, he was making connections between nature, art, culture, and architecture that eventually gave him a foundation for thinking about design.

To learn from Le Corbusier's creative search and to see how he evolved as an architect, one must understand where he started. He never attended a university or enrolled formally in an architecture school. His architectural training was mostly self-imposed and was heavily influenced by the teachings of his secondary-school tutor Charles L'Eplattenier, who taught him the fundamentals of drawing and the decorative arts at the École d'art in his hometown of La Chaux-de-Fonds in Swit-

Charles-Édouard Jeanneret, about 1910. FLC L4(1)140

zerland. Upon Jeanneret's graduation from secondary school in 1907, L'Eplattenier encouraged him to leave behind the rural landscapes and broaden his world view by making a formal drawing tour through northern Italy. This pedagogy of learning to draw and learning through experience was likely influenced by the long tradition of the Grand Tour, a rite of passage for European aristocrats. Travel was considered necessary to expand one's mind and understanding of the world. Architects, writers, and painters seized upon the idea, taking a standard itinerary across Europe to view monuments, antiquities, paintings, picturesque landscapes, and ancient cities.

The experience ignited in Jeanneret an enormous desire to see and understand other cultures and places through the architecture and urban space that shaped them. In Italy he expressed his first real interest in the built environment, primarily studying architectural details and building components. Shortly after his return, he set off again, for Vienna, Paris, and Germany, becoming increasingly interested in cityscapes and urban design. Periodically he returned home to recharge and reconnect with L'Eplattenier.

During his travels, the sketchbook emerged as Jeanneret's premier tool for recording and learning, and drawing became for him an essential and necessary medium of architectural training. Between 1902 and 1911 he produced hundreds of drawings, exploring a wide range of subject matter as well as means and methods of recording. With each trip he gained a broader view. As his interests shifted and expanded, so did his process of documenting what he saw. To his repertoire of perspective drawings of landscapes, beautifully detailed in watercolor, he added analytical sketches that captured the core of spatial forms and became a means of shorthand visual note taking. All the while, he frequently returned to old and familiar subjects to study them through different lenses in order to "see."

Giuliano Gresleri, architectural historian and author of *Les Voyages d'Allemagne: Carnets* and *Voyage d'Orient: Carnets* (which include reproductions of Jeanneret's notebooks during his travels to Germany and the East), said, "What distinguished Jeanneret's journey from those of his contemporaries at the École and from the tradition of the Grand Tour was precisely his awareness of 'being able to begin again.' Time and again, this notion stands out in the pages of his notebooks. The notes, the sketches, and the measurements were never ends in themselves, nor were they a part of the culture of the journey. They ceased being a diary and became design."

In 1911 Jeanneret completed the capstone of his informal education, a second drawing tour that Le Corbusier eventually coined his "Journey to the East" (actually the title of a book of essays and letters that he wrote during his travels there, published in 1966). By this time, he was interested in understanding more than just the monuments: he looked at the architecture and everyday culture. He had mastered the art of drawing through the daily practice of observing and recording what he saw. Through this rigorous exercise of learning to see, he had developed a vast tool kit of subject matter, means of authorship, drawing conventions (artistic and architectural), and media. More important, through drawing he came to understand the persistencies in architecture—color, form, light, shadow, structure, composition, mass, surface, context, proportion, and materials. As he reached Greece (halfway through his Journey to the East), Jeanneret not only proclaimed that he would become an architect but was working toward a theoretical position about design around which he could live and work.

L'Eplattenier was not the only influence on Le Corbusier's views of architectural theory and culture. In Paris he worked for the French architect Auguste Perret, who taught him to appreciate proportion, geometry, scale, harmony, and the classical language of architecture. In Germany, he met William Ritter, who would become another of Jeanneret's mentors and closest confidants. A music and art critic, intellectual, writer, and painter, Ritter exposed Jeanneret to new ideas in the art and architecture worlds. Indirectly Ritter led him to architect Peter Behrens (for whom he would work for several months in Germany), encouraged Jeanneret to experience the beauty of peasant life while traveling abroad, and inspired him to write. Jeanneret and Ritter corresponded through many letters, and Ritter constantly challenged Jeanneret to look beyond the comforts of La Chaux-de-Fonds and the more conservative views of L'Eplattenier.

While traveling to Germany, Jeanneret also discovered buildings by Theodor Fischer, a Munich-based architect and professor of urban planning. Jeanneret greatly admired his work and was also impressed by Fischer's aristocratic lifestyle. Though Fischer could not hire Jeanneret, he exposed him further to urban planning and reinforced the importance of geometric proportion in architectural design. In Germany Jeanneret also made friends with fellow painter August Klipstein. Thanks to their friendship, Jeanneret ultimately decided not to stay and work in Germany, but rather joined Klipstein as he traveled East. Their lively discussions on the road further allowed Jeanneret to flesh out his developing architectural ideals.

In the end, however, travel drawing was Jeanneret's education and his rite of passage. Embodied in his sketchbooks is an incredibly comprehensive means of visual exploration and discovery. Though he never had a formal architectural education, his intense curiosity to understand the world through drawing and painting and writing is what made him such a dynamic architect, one from whom we can still learn today. The lessons he learned formed the basis of his general outlook and provided content for his later seminal text, *Vers une architecture*. They also prepared him to become Le Corbusier.

Range and Evolution of Subject Matter

One expects most architects in training to go out and draw buildings. Jeanneret, however, was curious about everything. While his primary focus shifted from trip to trip, he drew flora, fauna, people, objects, art, patterns, and furniture, as well as landscapes, cityscapes, interior

Landscapes (Jura forest, pencil and watercolor, 13 x 14.8 cm. FLC 2111)

and urban space, facades, architectural and construction details, monuments, and everyday architecture.

Nonetheless, each time period can be broadly defined by distinct interests and subjects of study. When learning to draw in La Chaux-de-Fonds, he looked primarily at the natural world, drawing landscapes, flora and fauna, geometries and patterns related to the decorative arts.

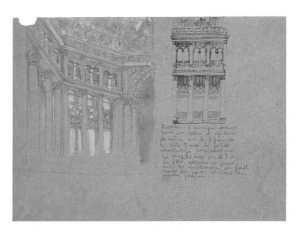

Objects (Boat, Cabourg, France, watercolor, 35.5 x 53.5 cm. FLC 4068)

Cityscapes/urban space (Basilica and Vatican walls, Rome, 1911, pencil and colored pencil. *Voyage d'Orient*, Carnet 4, p. 135.)

Architectural details (Interior of Baptistery, Florence, 1907, pencil, ink and watercolor, 25.2 x 35.1 cm. FLC 2172)

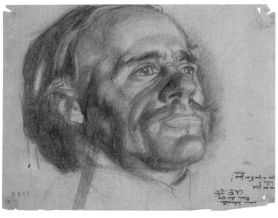

People (Portrait of Schneider, pencil, 21.2 x 27.3 cm. FLC 1988)

During his first formal drawing trip, to Italy, he continued exploring the decorative arts by drawing the surface and ornament of building components—mainly objects as opposed to places.

When he arrived in Vienna and Paris, his interest shifted to interiors, to medieval urbanism, and to cityscapes as landscapes. In Germany he studied public squares, urban spaces, and the iconic buildings that anchored them. By the time he set off on his Journey to the East, he had enlarged his attention to the culture and urban spaces of the entire city, as if he were seeing it from ten thousand feet above. Yet his youthful curiosities remained: he drew peasants' houses, people, food, simple pots, plants, animals, insects, and furniture.

General Methods/Processes

Jeanneret relied on four different methods for approaching his subject matter. Not all of his drawings fit exactly into these categories, but they are useful for purposes of analysis:

    Representational drawings
    Representational drawings with a level of
        abstraction
    Analytical drawings
    Visual note taking/diagramming

Representational drawings are drawings that render the world exactly as one sees it. Representational drawings with a level of abstraction suggest that the author is interpreting what he or she sees—simplifying details or exaggerating color, for example, so that the viewer can identify the beginnings of an idea behind the work.

Analytical drawings, in contrast, are used to unpack or break down what one sees so as to better understand its elements, tease out new concepts, or provide new interpretations of the subject matter. Visual note taking or diagramming typically is a reminder to the author of what is important to "take away"—forms, space, proportion, to name a few elements.

Throughout his formative years Jeanneret made representational drawings and paintings. However, during this time he learned to see objects not only for what they were but also for the larger ideas that they embodied. He did not ask, "What is it that I am looking at?" but instead, "what is this doing or telling me?" As a result, he was able to make *purposeful* drawings that expressed a clear and specific understanding of the subject matter. By choosing whether a drawing was about the picturesque or about the geometry of evergreen trees, or about the conceptual link between the two, he gave the drawing a position, or something to say. From this moment of

Representational drawing (Jura barn in landscape, October 15, 1902, pencil and watercolor on paper, 12 x 16 cm. FLC 2185)

Representation with a level of abstraction (Mountains, pencil and watercolor, 16.2 x 19.5 cm. FLC 2033)

departure he could then decide on the most appropriate drawing convention and medium to use to best convey a certain point of view.

In essence, as Jeanneret approached the work using these different methods, he was exercising varying degrees of authorship. This becomes evident when you look at a photograph of what Jeanneret was observing as opposed to what he chose to draw. There are too many details to capture what we actually see in the real world; as Jeanneret became more adept at making drawings, he learned to make decisions about the lines that mattered,

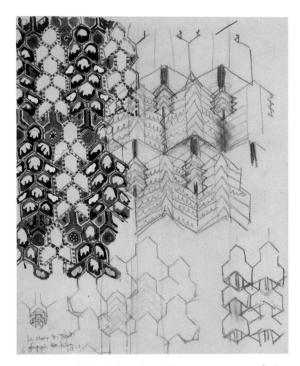

ABOVE: Analytical drawing (Abstract pattern of pine tree, La Chaux-de-Fonds, 1907, pencil, watercolor, and gouache, 27.2 x 21.2 cm. FLC 1763) RIGHT: Visual note taking/diagramming (Piazza Navona, Rome, 1911, pencil, *Voyage d'Orient*, Carnet 4, p. 150.)

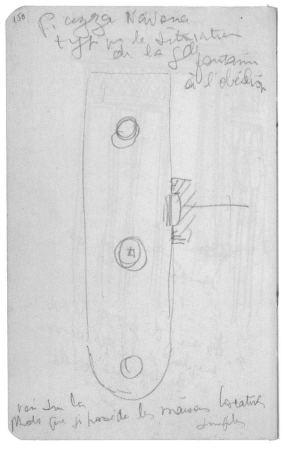

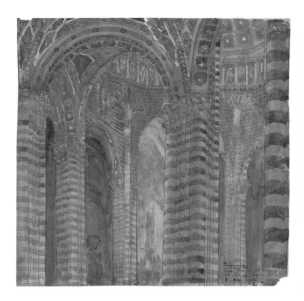

LEFT: Interior of the cathedral, Siena, October 5, 1907, pencil and watercolor on paper pasted on cardboard, 21 x 20.6 cm. FLC 2465 ABOVE: Photo: Jacob Brillhart

choosing by design those that he would draw and those that he would leave out.

In the *representational drawing* of the interior of the cathedral in Siena, Jeanneret chose to depict the space: you can almost feel what it would be like to be inside. He is getting after only a few aspects of the experience, focusing on the play of light on atmosphere, materials, and color. If you compare the drawing to the photograph, you can see that he paints the space an exaggerated ultramarine blue. He varies the color and value throughout the drawing; for instance, the surface of the horizontal bands is never even or one solid color. This gives an excellent sense of reality, since in real life we never perceive a surface or wall in unvarying color and value.

The central space is the main subject of the study. By eliminating the ground plane, Jeanneret increases the scale of the space and eliminates the tremendous sense of weight that exists in real life. The increased scale and intensity of light emphasize the vertical expanse. Knowing not to draw everything, he blurs the details in the deep perspective moments between the columns, giving focus only to the foreground and increasing the level of detail as he moves towards the upper edge of the sheet. In doing so, he allows the viewer's eye to rest and to move around, in and out of the drawing, with varying focus. This technique gives the viewer a changing visual experience and allows us to imagine what the space looks like, rather than providing us with a highly representational picture that offers equal detail and focus throughout.

This *analytical drawing* of the same cathedral in Siena clearly reveals Jeanneret's interest in the architectural ingredients of the facade. Here the lines that he chooses to draw show that he is paying attention to surface conditions—materials and textures, the marble pattern, the facade's proportional system and its composition and the rhythm of bays, as well as the carved details of the stone columns and pedestals. Documented here is also the profile—the complex roofscape—of the building, heightened by a dark sepia wash that blocks out the sky.

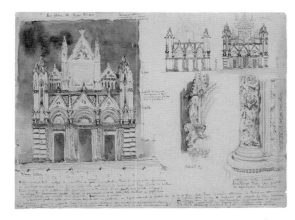

Cathedral facade and details, Siena, 1907, pencil, ink, and watercolor on paper, 25.5 x 34.5 cm. FLC 6055

Photo: Jacob Brillhart

Jeanneret has left quite a lot out of the drawing. The drawing does not convey the dramatic, heightened perspective that a viewer feels when standing in front of the cathedral. The choice of a flattened orthographic elevation rather than a perspectival drawing signals that here he is not interested in urban space and context. He does not draw what is in front of the church—the large public space, the front steps, passersby (not even one figure for scale)—and he eliminates the colors (pinks, golds, blues, and greens) of the scene. The door details are simplified and the rose window and bell tower in the distance are left out.

By the time Jeanneret made the drawing of the Pantheon in Rome in 1911, he had perfected his shorthand visual note-taking method. In fact, there are more than six pages of notes and sketches of the building in his sketchbooks. The upward forced perspective captures the urban experience of walking up to and around the Pantheon (a necessary vantage point because of the closely surrounding medieval fabric). The study depicts the connection of the two main exterior components of

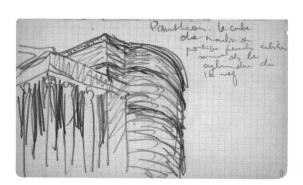

The Pantheon, Rome, 1911, pencil, *Voyage d'Orient*, Carnet 5, p. 13.

Photo: Jacob Brillhart

the building—the drum and the portico—and analyzes their shape and form.

Here color, texture, the material change from brick to stone, and the light source are omitted, as is the context of the medieval surroundings. The elaborate Corinthian capitals are reduced to simple loops at the top of each column.

Drawing Types

Graphics are the means through which architects present their ideas. Typically, they explore design concepts by making orthographic, scaled drawings such as plans, sections, and elevations that delineate buildings in two-dimensional form. A floor plan is essentially an aerial diagram that shows the layout and arrangement of space of a particular level of building; an elevation is a flattened drawing of a building's facade; and a section is an imagined view that would be created if one were to cut through a building vertically, revealing interior elevations and adjacencies of rooms across all levels (often showing detailed construction assemblies through walls as well).

In addition to plans, sections, and elevations, Jeanneret also made many other types of drawings that enabled him to understand buildings in three-dimensional form. He drew axonometric projections, depicting buildings in a way that would reveal more than one facade at a time. He drew landscape, architectural, and street perspectives—views that exhibit the way one actually perceives the environment in real life. He made bird's-eye drawings, rendering buildings and urban spaces in perspective as if seen from above, and fish-eye views, which gave a convex, hemispherical appearance to his subjects of study. He also annotated his drawings extensively.

Though he did make some early diagrammatic studies, his first drawing conventions by and large more closely resembled those of an artist, depicting landscapes and architectural details in perspective. From his time in Vienna, he began to explore conventional architectural representation (plans, sections, and elevations), and thereafter he showed a growing facility with more complex architectural projections. He introduced plans and diagrams of urban spaces as a type of documentation in

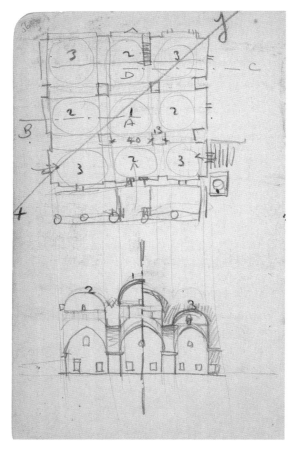

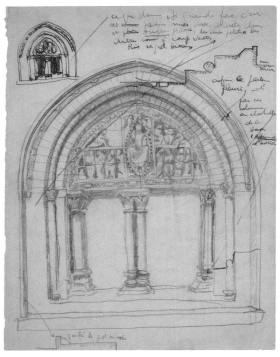

LEFT: Plan and section (Eski Jami Mosque, Adrianople, Bursa, 1911, pencil and colored pencil, *Voyage d'Orient*, Carnet 2, p. 56.) ABOVE: Elevation (Romanesque window detail, Carennac, France, pencil and ink, 31.5 x 24 cm. FLC 1909)

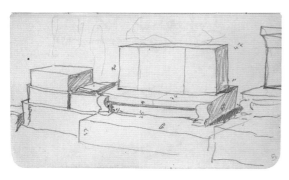

Axonometric (Ruins, Greece, 1911, pencil, *Voyage d'Orient*, Carnet 3, p. 151.)

Landscape perspective (Landscape and lake, 1905, watercolor, 12.2 x 17.3 cm. FLC 1746)

Street perspective (Street view, Constantinople, 1911, pencil on paper. FLC 2457)

Bird's-eye view (View of Turnovo, Bulgaria, June 1911, pencil on paper, 12 x 20 cm. FLC 2496)

Germany. Finally, by the time of his Journey to the East, he was deploying all the drawing conventions. However, the rationale behind *what* convention he used is more interesting than the actual *range* of conventions utilized. Thus, he deployed different types of drawings to clearly convey his ideas. For example, he used bird's-eye views to capture the city and fish-eye views to portray the interior of a cafe. He also produced simplified and highly diagrammatic plans, sections, and perspectives to get at the essence of a place.

ABOVE: Fish-eye view (Café of Mahmoud Pacha, 1911, pencil on paper, 13 x 19.3 cm. FLC 1880)
RIGHT: Diagram (Plan of the Green Mosque, Bursa, 1911, pencil, *Voyage d'Orient*, Carnet 3, p. 19.)

Technique and Media

While certain themes emerged during each time period or trip, it is almost impossible to systematically categorize Jeanneret's drawing evolution over time: this is what makes studying his drawings so interesting. In the pages of this book you can see the complexity of his creative search, as he continually wove together different subjects with different media at different times in order to learn to see in order to know. By the time he made what became known as his Journey to the East, he also had a camera at his disposal, adding to the means with which he documented the world. Nonetheless, he still felt the camera was "a tool for idlers" and predominantly relied on the following to capture his surroundings:

Media
• Pencil only
• Watercolor (with little to no pencil)
• Watercolor/gouache and pencil
• Pencil, ink, and watercolor
• Pencil and colored pencil

Surfaces
• Loose sheets of watercolor paper
• Sketchbooks (some blank, some with graph paper)
• Miscellaneous (for example, the backs of postcards he picked up during his travels)

When Jeanneret was first learning to draw, he was interested in making beautiful paintings that depicted the world as he saw it, in perspective. Watercolor, which expresses the range of color and subtleties of value that exist in the real world, was his primary medium: the aqueous paint moves over the sheet and deposits the color in an irregular or organic way that mimics what the eye actually perceives. Concerned with making *paintings*, Jeanneret drew in very quickly (although with remarkable accuracy) the pencil base-line work before applying watercolor washes. The pencil lines delineated the most important edges and geometries, which were then filled with paint to convey color, pattern, and surface. Dwelling on the picturesque in Italy, his pencil line work became much more detailed, while his mastery of watercolor reached its peak. Continuing primarily to use watercolor in Vienna and Paris, his studies grew quicker and looser.

Throughout his trips, Jeanneret worked on loose sheets of watercolor paper, generally 16 x 20 cm (about 6¼ x 7⅞ inches), except when drawing complete buildings with details; then he worked on larger sheets measuring 25 x 32 cm (9⅞ x 12⅝ inches). However, it appears that he began to use sketchbooks in Paris. In Germany Jeanneret needed to cover a lot of ground quickly: he wanted to see many of the country's town centers as well as study other schools' teaching of the decorative arts (as part of a research grant he obtained from the École d'art in La Chaux-de-Fonds). This is when sketchbooks (*carnets*, as he called them) became his main sur-

ABOVE: Watercolor only, on loose sheet of paper (Stylized study of forest, watercolor, 18.3 x 16.3 cm. FLC 2519) RIGHT: Watercolor with heavy pencil work on loose sheet of paper (Building with turret in Fribourg, about 1907, watercolor and pencil, 17.8 x 12 cm. FLC 2076)

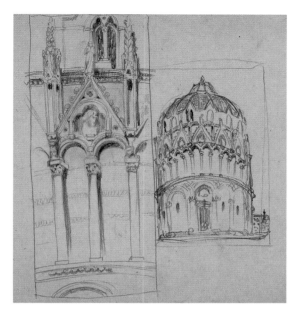

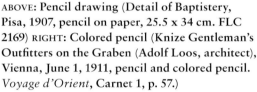

ABOVE: Pencil drawing (Detail of Baptistery, Pisa, 1907, pencil on paper, 25.5 x 34 cm. FLC 2169) RIGHT: Colored pencil (Knize Gentleman's Outfitters on the Graben (Adolf Loos, architect), Vienna, June 1, 1911, pencil and colored pencil. *Voyage d'Orient*, Carnet 1, p. 57.)

face type. Smaller in size, some with graph paper, these books were ideal for note taking and quick sketches. He also began to use the backs of postcards for sketches and notes, occasionally returning to do drawings on loose paper. Making very quick drawings, he mostly used pencil, though sometimes a combination of pencil, ink, and watercolor.

In his last drawing tour, the Journey to the East, Jeanneret produced hundreds of drawings. Most were very fast pen-and-pencil sketches, which often were punctuated with colored pencil, but he also continued to do watercolors.

Study of leaves, pencil and watercolor on paper, 11.5 x 12.8 cm. FLC 1740

La Chaux-de-Fonds, Switzerland

Jeanneret spent five years (1902–1907) learning the basics of drawing in his hometown of La Chaux-de-Fonds, in the Jura Mountain region of Switzerland. While at the École d'art (which trained locals in decorative design and engraving for the city's watchmaking industry), he studied under the intimate tutelage of Charles L'Eplattenier, who would deeply influence his life and his development as an architect. L'Eplattenier taught Jeanneret the most fundamental drawing skills—observing and realistically documenting a chosen subject. Although Jeanneret was naturally talented from a very early age, he made the practice of representational drawing in situ a daily ritual.

Jeanneret's primary focus of study was the natural world. The surrounding Jura Mountains were a spectacular source of beauty and inspiration, and the study of nature was integral to the teachings of the École. Not only was nature a passion of L'Eplattenier's, but it was also at the core of John Ruskin's writings, including *The Seven Lamps of Architecture*; Owen Jones's *Grammar of Ornament* (which said that art is the idealization of natural forms and ornament should be based on the structural growth of natural forms); and the larger influence of art nouveau, all of which were part of the school's decorative-design curriculum.

In his earliest years at the École, Jeanneret painted beautifully detailed and picturesque watercolors of scenic rural vistas, forests, flora, fauna, and objects in the landscape, and, periodically, people. Most of his drawings were highly representational and perspectival; the aesthetic beauty of the subjects was prioritized above all else. Interest in larger architectural principles was absent, but these works were rich in material feeling and showed a clear understanding of space, depth, and color.

Jeanneret also learned to use a certain level of abstraction in paintings that revealed a growing sense of artistic exploration and a shift away from pure documentation. The school's course of study about decorative design and the composition of ornament stressed color, pattern, solid and void, geometries and form. Nature was a spring point for design. Through these courses, Jeanneret produced a series of analytical drawings of objects in the natural world. Unlike his representational drawings, where he would produce one image per loose sheet of paper, he would make multiple analytical sketches per page. He built his analytical drawings primarily using soft pencil and pen.

In the last two years at the École, Jeanneret was enrolled in the school's Cours Supérieur, which focused on architecture. Nature continued to serve as a point of departure; he made numerous studies of rock strata and trees to inform his architectural designs and details.

This period of Jeanneret's life provided the educational underpinnings to his artistic search and must be studied in order to understand his development as both an artist and an architect. His early analysis of nature, in particular, allowed him to distill and extract larger ideas about his subject matter. The ability to edit and analyze is arguably the most important and fundamental skill that an architect can have. His developing competency is what eventually enabled him to get to the crux of an idea, whether about buildings, urban spaces, cities, art, or culture generally. It led directly to design drawing.

In Jeanneret's first year of school, he was required to redraw details from Owen Jones's *Grammar of Ornament*; below is Jeanneret's copy of a plate of Egyptian ornament done in pencil with red, blue, green, gray, black, white, orange, and yellow watercolor.

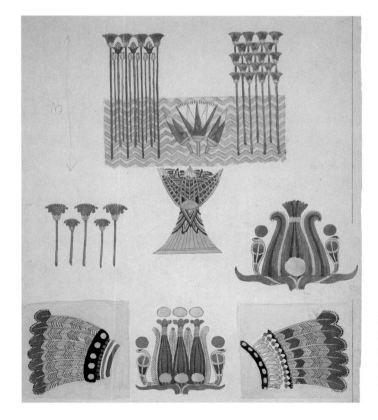

Egyptian ornament taken from Owen Jones's *Grammar of Ornament*, pencil and watercolor, 32.5 x 24.7 cm. FLC 1779

Barn in landscape, Jura, October 15, 1902, pencil and watercolor on paper, 12 x 16 cm. FLC 2185

La Chaux-de-Fonds is defined by its rolling hills, sweeping vistas, and dense pine-tree forests. The area's spectacular natural beauty was of prime importance to the people of the region, and Jeanneret spent much of his early childhood outdoors. The characteristic farmsteads with low-pitched roofs would remain an iconic image for Jeanneret. He painted this watercolor drawing, a picturesque, highly representational image in a perspective view, with multiple layers of watercolor and very little pencil work, during his first year at the École, when he was fifteen years old.

Interior, 1904, pencil,
watercolor, and gouache on
paper, 17.8 x 16.2 cm. FLC
2186

Jeanneret explores the interplay of light and architecture, using the window, a primary architectural (and artistic) device. The glare illuminates the tablecloth, depicted with a quick layer of gouache. This drawing reveals Jeanneret's understanding of color theory: he uses alternating warm and cool colors from foreground to background to give a sense of space, while the complementary bluish purple and yellow-ochre tones create color harmony. The composition is a one-point perspective, directing the viewer's eye toward a single point along the "horizon line," a drawing device that allows objects to appear far away. Here the horizon line is depicted as the tree-line in the distance, beyond the window pane.

Girl playing the violin, pencil and gouache on paper, 19.5 x 12.5 cm. FLC 1993

Woman sewing, pencil and gouache on paper, 15 x 17.3 cm. FLC 2205

Two compositions with the human form; in one, to set up the drawing Jeanneret made a small diagrammatic vignette organizing the hierarchy of main ideas by accenting in color the woman's headdress and the violin. Both of these drawings combine figural and man-made objects and are painted like traditional still lifes.

Sketches of lizards, colored pencil and watercolor on paper, 25 x 32.4 cm. FLC 2524

Two sheets of figural positions, above and opposite: the exercise of drawing something in motion forces one to draw quickly and to draw only the essential lines as opposed to the details. The gestural quality, as well as the range of the pencil line work (going from dark to light, with some lizards drawn in lightly, others with bolder lines, and some fully painted) reinforces the idea of movement, time, and sequence. Note that Jeanneret draws the lizards from above (orthographically); in profile (elevation); and perspectivally, capturing them in numerous positions.

Sketches of lizards, colored pencil and watercolor on paper, 25 x 36 cm. FLC 1966

The two perspective drawings (overleaf) are traditional landscapes. Both are broken into multiple zones; use a "device" to lead the viewer's eye through the drawing; include varying levels of detail and contrast; and rely on multiple layers of depth, color, and value. Jeanneret divided the farmland composition into four zones: the foreground is highly detailed, while the middle ground of fields is represented mostly through texture, pattern, and form organized by three diagonal roads that draw the eye deeper into the work. The background, which provides a buffer between skyscape and ground plane, is

Farmland, pencil, watercolor, and gouache on paper, 20.7 x 14.8 cm. FLC 1752

Landscape, pencil, watercolor, and gouache on paper, 20.7 x 28.3 cm. FLC 1922

undeveloped and checkered with a few buildings to add
scale and context; because it depicts forest, this zone also
offers the greatest level of contrast. If the viewer squints at
the drawing, this moment of trees meeting sky is the most
definitive and where the painting opens up to allow for an
infinite vista. The sky is a last layer of depth, color, and
value, moving from ochre to blue.

Similarly, the landscape painting has a foreground,
middle ground, and background, linked by the river that
runs diagonally through the painting. The river leads the
viewer's eye into the distance, which eventually merges
with the sky.

Landscape, pencil, watercolor, and gouache on paper, 23.9 x 30.6 cm. FLC 1762

These expressive landscapes evoke a sense of atmosphere through exaggerated color, perspective, and composition. With little pencil work and bold paint application, these drawings allow one to see the natural landscape in its abstracted form.

In the forest scene, Jeanneret flattens the foreground and background to make one plane. In contrast, the landscape painting above has a sense of depth and an extended vista with foreground, middle ground, background, and horizon.

Forest, pencil, watercolor, and gouache on paper, 18.2 x 11.5 cm. FLC 2043

Jura landscape, pencil and watercolor on paper, 13.5 x 12.3 cm. FLC 2100

View to the outdoors, pencil, watercolor, and gouache on yellow paper, 8.7 x 10.5 cm. FLC 2202

Jeanneret continues to reduce intricate natural landscapes to simplified forms while placing emphasis on composition. These landscapes are less about moving the viewer's eye through the drawing. The Jura landscape drawing is more about form and pattern than it is a literal representation; in the view to the outdoors, the landscape is framed by a window that organizes the scene and allows a great depth of field. Again, in masterly fashion Jeanneret obtains visual depth by drawing the interior of the window mullion and then dividing the landscape into three layers at different scales—red flowers, yellow trees, and blue hillside, clouds, and snow-covered mountains beyond, at the horizon line.

Flower studies, pencil and watercolor on paper, 13.7 x 13.7 cm. FLC 2107

Study of a flower, pencil and watercolor on paper, 25 x 36 cm. FLC 5856

Side by side these two drawings clearly express Jeanneret's expansive interests—art and the rigorous analysis of decorative design. One is a "painterly" approach in which he depicts the flower in context, using bold watercolors. The other drawing explores flower parts from different vantage points, without context and with a limited amount of paint used purely as a means of documentation. This kind of analysis was central to Jeanneret's studies during the first three years of school.

Combining the approaches deployed in the preceding flower illustrations: this is a hybrid painting—a traditional landscape through an analytical lens. The beginnings of what the landscape *could* be begin to manifest themselves. Trees pose as objects geometrically simplified as cones and understood as form and color. Warmer green tones are used in the foreground and middle ground and cool blues in the distance. Bold forms are reinforced through repetition. In contrast, the sky plays a lesser role. The white, snowy gouache swaths move the eye around and through the cones. The transition from blue to green to orange to green, from background to foreground, is a telling mark of Jeanneret's color mastery.

Trees in field, pencil, watercolor, and gouache on paper, 8.5 x 13 cm. FLC 2204

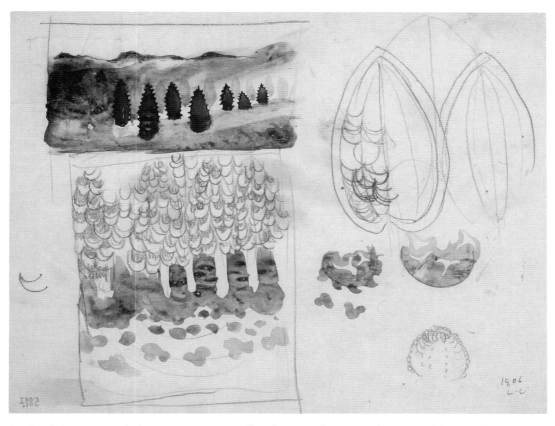

Study of pine trees and pinecones, 1906, pencil and watercolor on tracing paper, 21.2 x 27.4 cm.
FLC 5817

The powerful sketches overleaf create a visual bridge
between representational art and organic design strate-
gies. While most of the drawings made during Jeanneret's
training at the École are undated, the dated study above
is a rare exception and indicates that he was in his fourth
year when he made it. Given the similarities in style, we
can assume the others were made at the same time. Jeanneret here begins to break down the landscape and mine
it for its formal geometries. The top left of the drawing
above is a thumbnail watercolor perspective sketch of
the Jura hillside, and the trees are reduced to blue cones

Pinecone study, ink, pencil, and gouache, 21.3 x 27.5 cm. FLC 1775

(very similar to the drawing on page 54). Then, on the right of the same sheet, Jeanneret changes scale, reducing the landscape to the scale and form of a single pinecone. This is his first act of deduction and abstraction through drawing. At the bottom left of the sheet, below the blue thumbnail sketch, he notes the growth—i.e., the multiplied number of pinecones—covering the trees.

In the ink drawings above and opposite, he explores structure, skin, and materiality, flattening the forms into

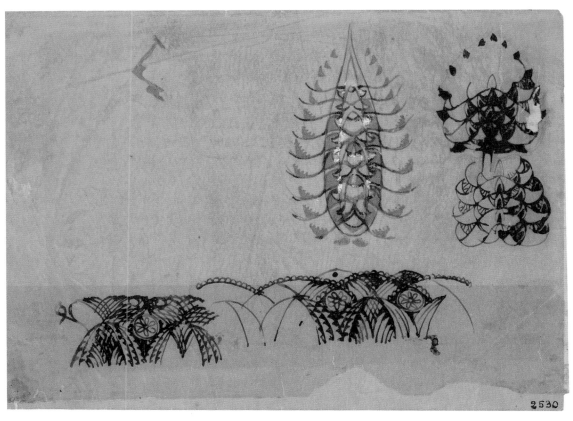

Pinecone study, ink, pencil, and gouache on tracing paper, 18.8 x 25.8 cm. FLC 2530-V

patterns and geometric fields that can be translated into decorative details. (Here color is used to emphasize pattern, symmetry, and repetition.) In the sketch opposite, the symmetrical nature of the pinecone becomes clear; he only sketches half of it. He investigates its layering, physical nesting, and growth characteristics. In the third sketch, he draws the pinecone architecturally— in section—exploring the interior skeletal frame of the structure.

Flower study, pencil and watercolor on paper, 23.7 x 14.6 cm. FLC 2206

Evergreen trees, Switzerland, 1906/1907, India ink and pencil on paper, 15.3 x 17.3 cm. FLC 2520

Four sketches (pages 60–63) show the abstraction of flora as a means of exploring pattern making. Rather than depicting nature literally, Jeanneret simplifies the flowers (opposite) by expressing the geometries of the leaves and the colors of the flowers; above, and over-leaf, the evergreen trees are abstracted into tiled fields and patterns in the two tree sketches. Tiled patterns like those in the fourth drawing inform designs he made both for watchcases (in his design classes) and for villas (when he was enrolled in the Cours Supérieur).

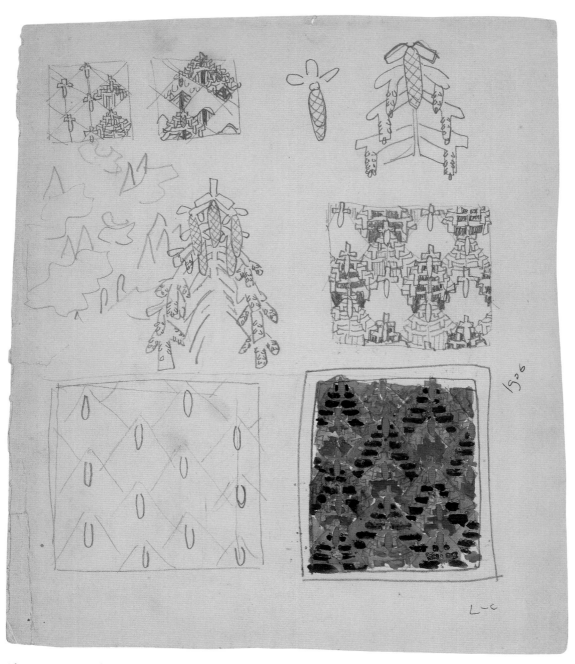

Abstract patterns based on evergreen trees, 1906, pencil and watercolor on paper, 26.5 x 22.6 cm. FLC 5822

Geometric pattern studies, pencil, watercolor and gouache, 24.3 x 31.7 cm. FLC 1765

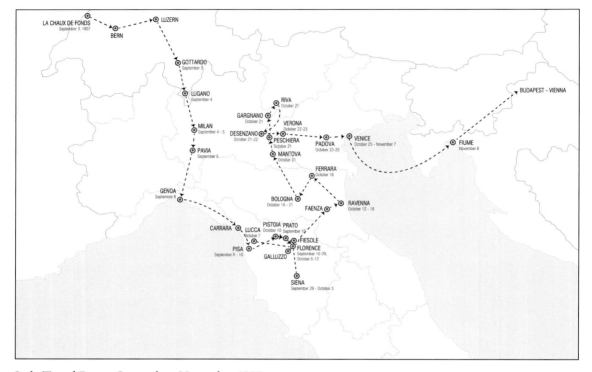

Italy Travel Route: September–November 1907

Italy

When Jeanneret graduated from the École, L'Eplattenier encouraged him to learn more about the great architecture of the past. The nineteen-year-old embarked with his classmate Léon Perrin on a two-and-half month tour of northern Italy in 1907. Like many travelers of the day, Jeanneret used Baedeker's travel guidebook and often turned to Hippolyte Taine's *Voyage en Italie*. Many historians suggest that he may also have followed John Ruskin's travel itineraries: he drew many of the same Gothic buildings Ruskin described in *Les Matins à Florence* and *Stones of Venice*.

In this first formal drawing tour, Jeanneret remained interested primarily in the picturesque; however, rather than sketching the natural world, he set off to study architectural details and buildings in the city. He focused largely on pre-Renaissance buildings and art, bypassing much of the great Renaissance work of Bramante, Brunelleschi, Palladio, and others. The cathedrals of Pisa and Milan, the Doge's Palace and St. Mark's in Venice, and the Palazzo Vecchio, Orsanmichele, and Bargello courtyard in Florence drew his attention.

Coming from the world of decorative arts, Jeanneret approached the built environment by looking at the micro; moving from building detail to building detail, sculpture to sculpture, and painting to painting. Less interested in mass or form, he mainly drew surface and ornament in architecture—facades, frescos, mosaics, pavement patterns, and architectural details such as capitals, pediments, and corner details, as well as window-to-wall relationships. His interest in surface would later serve as one of the foundations of *Vers une architecture*, in which he explains the necessity of surface and articulation as primary elements of good design.

Like many of his earlier drawings, where he was mainly interested in making beautiful paintings, Jeanneret's Italy studies were often representational in nature. However, he did make a number of analytical drawings, such as those that unpacked the components of a facade. With both approaches, he relied on flattened elevational compositions or two-point-perspective drawings of architectural corners (where the construction lines of each abutting face vanish at two different points—and in opposite directions—on the page.) Very few of the drawings depict *space* in perspective or in plan.

Jeanneret made more than fifty sketches on loose sheets of paper during his time in Italy. He spent more time in front of his subjects here than he would on any later trip—following the tradition of the Grand Tour by laboriously and meticulously documenting details and studying building composition. Unlike the method used in his earlier watercolor drawings in Switzerland, here he dedicated an extensive amount of time to forming the base line work of the drawing using a sharp (but soft) lead pencil. In some drawings, he would use the pencil to color in the shadows before adding the first watercolor wash, which would seal the lead into the sheet and keep the line work crisp and permanent. Rather than relying on a dry-brush technique, he wet the brush before going to the paint, so that he made medium-wet to wet strokes when applying the initial washes. He would generally apply at least three layers of color and sometimes also gouache, to increase opacity. To prevent the watercolor from becoming overly muddy or too blurred, it appears that he often allowed the previous washes to dry before applying a new wash. A number of his analytical drawings were done solely in pencil; however, what is most striking about the drawings from this trip is his absolute mastery of watercolor technique.

Details of the facade of the Cathedral of Pisa, 1907, pencil on paper, 25.4 x 34 cm. FLC 5837

Facade details, Baptistery,
Pisa, 1907, pencil on paper,
25.5 x 34 cm. FLC 2169

On September 3, 1907, Jeanneret left La Chaux-de-Fonds by train, to make his way to Florence. Traveling alone, he made brief day stops to sightsee in Lugano, Milan, Pavia, and Genoa. On September 6 he arrived in Pisa, where he remained for four days, studying the Cathedral, the Baptistery, and neighboring Campo Santo with its frescoes.

Jeanneret's ability to unpack the Cathedral's architectural details analytically, as shown in this early sketch of the facade, is impressive for a nineteen-year-old with no formal architectural training. The drawing begins to incorporate ideas of facade structure and its direct relationship to decoration and ornamentation. He highlights many geometrical intricacies and subtle rhythm shifts of column heights and widths, moving the viewer's eye around to the points of interest in the structure. (Later in the trip, he made a similar but more painterly drawing of the facade of the San Martino Cathedral in Lucca (see page 91).

Sketch of beggars in *Triumph over Death* by Buonamico Buffalmacco, a mid-fourteenth-century fresco on the south wall of Campo Santo at Pisa, pencil on paper, 11.9 x 16.5 cm. FLC 2167

Still unsure whether he wanted to be an artist or an architect, Jeanneret copied frescoes. Perhaps his interest in drawing art was derived from the teachings of Ruskin and Taine, who stressed the importance in understanding composition as it pertained to both sculpture and paintings. With his interest in pre-Renaissance buildings, the Cathedral of Pisa must have been an excellent site to draw. With the first stone laid in 1093, the building is a spectacular example of Pisan Romanesque architecture, with a distinctive pastel-colored marble facade and four rows of arcades and arches reminiscent of Moorish architecture. Scholar Geoffrey Baker pointed out that Ruskin praised the Cathedral in *The Seven Lamps of Architecture* for its perfect architectural arrangement. The Campo Santo is the large Gothic cloister located at the northern end of the Cathedral square.

Cathedral of Pisa, King
David, September 1907,
pencil, watercolor, and
gouache on paper, 24.8 x
13.6 cm. FLC 5861

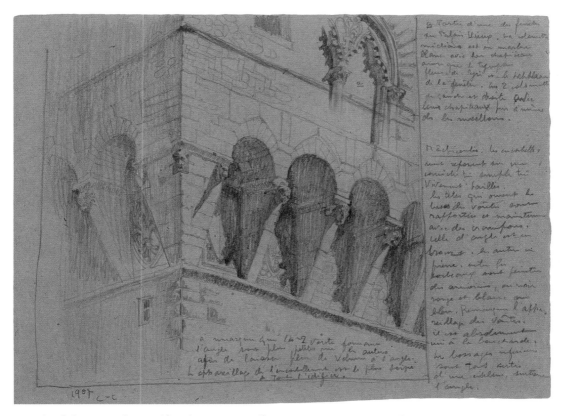

Details of the Torre di Arnolfo, Florence, pencil on paper, 19 x 25 cm. FLC 5846

In addition to analytical studies, Jeanneret also made impressionistic paintings. The drawing of the statue of King David highlights the details of the filigree of the niche. The complex layering of watercolor washes creates visual depth, conveys surface variability, and offers a compelling sense of the range of the surface's color, value, and texture.

When Jeanneret intended to depict form, he relied on pencil value rather than watercolor, to keep attention on the somber, solid, muted nature of the building, as in his drawing of the Torre di Arnolfo (otherwise known as the Tower of Palazzo Vecchio). When he did use watercolor to express form, it was generally subtle and used to highlight value.

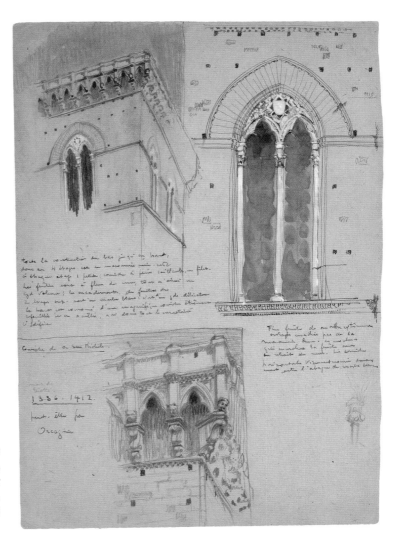

Exterior of the
Orsanmichele, Florence,
pencil, ink, and watercolor
on paper, 36 x 25.4 cm.
FLC 2083

The Orsanmichele is a Romanesque building built in 1336 and noted for its exquisite vaulting and brickwork. The exterior niches were designed to house the patron saints from each of the major guilds. Originally designed as a market, the first floor of the building became a church in 1380. Jeanneret drew details of the tabernacle, built 1348–1359 by Orcagna, to frame Bernardo Daddi's *Madonna and Child*; see page 72.)

Interior of Orsanmichele, Florence, September 1907, pencil and watercolor on paper, 34.5 x 25.5 cm. FLC 2265

Jeanneret clearly understood how different media and drawing conventions could most appropriately convey and capture his subject of focus. Opposite, he deploys ink and pencil to explore exterior details—skin, surface, window and cornice details, rendered in perspective and elevation. The drawing (above) of the interior, in perspective, uses bold watercolor washes to express space, the groin vaults, and color.

Tabernacle detail (design by Andrea Orcagna) at Orsanmichele, Florence, pencil and watercolor on paper, 14.5 x 12 cm. FLC 1983

Essentially plan drawings, these are reminiscent of Jeanneret's studies of geometry, pattern, and ornament made at the École d'art. He uses an intense underlay of pencil work, drawing every line of the pattern, and deploys a very sophisticated watercolor technique that is not easy to execute. Looking at the continuous filigree work in the drawing of the Baptistery pavement—the rectilinear borders and the snaking verti-

Pavement detail, Baptistery, Florence, 1907, pencil and watercolor on paper pasted on cardboard, 16 x 17 cm. FLC 2164

cal lines—one might imagine that in reality these stone lines are a solid color with consistent value. In the drawing, however, the colors change from blue to purple to pink to green to blue, and from orange to green and back. This mixing of different colors (and values) rather than applying a flat, solid color is what gives the work a lifelike quality. It captures the way actual light is always changing across surfaces.

Niche housing
Donatello's statue
of Saint Mark,
Orsanmichele, Florence,
October 9, 1907, pencil,
gouache, and watercolor,
31.3 x 15.7 cm. FLC 2162

Exterior wall tombs, Santa Maria Novella, Florence, October 1907, watercolor, gouache, pencil, and black ink on paper, 22 x 19 cm. FLC 5845

We start to see Jeanneret's authorship at play in these two perspective drawings. He does not draw everything (he dissolves the context and blurs the image of Saint Mark; in the painting of Santa Maria Novella, he is clearly depicting the wall tombs and not the context). He is telling us that he is more interested in the details of the architectural niche than he is in the figure it houses. What he does not draw also lends a bit of mystery to each place.

When Jeanneret's drawings were about pattern (as on the preceding pages), he used a lot of watercolor. When they were about the play of light and dark, he was careful not to render what was in shadow. His drawings, rather than looking flat, expressed form in three dimensions and displayed the depth and hard geometries found in his subjects. In analyzing form and light through drawing, he began to understand architecture as dynamic and temporal.

Detail of Spanish Chapel in Santa Maria Novella, Florence, October 1907, pencil and watercolor on paper, 23.7 x 23.5 cm. FLC 2037

These two drawings reveal Jeanneret's interests in interiors. The above image highlights the ornamental detailing of the filigree ironwork (again captured with a lot of color to denote pattern). In the second image, he shifts his focus away from the architecture of the interior wall to the art on the wall in the fresco painting *Passion of Our Lord*.

Detail of Christ carrying the cross, from the fourteenth-century fresco *Passion of Our Lord* by Andrea di Bonaiuto, in the Spanish Chapel, Florence, pencil, watercolor, and gouache on paper, 20.7 x 15.9 cm. FLC 1971

Santa Croce, Florence, 1907, pencil and watercolor on ivory paper, 24 x 32.5 cm. FLC 2175

These drawings show Jeanneret's ability to look at many things within a single space. We see him shift his attention from construction assemblies in the above drawing to the fine art within the same space, at right. Notably, the first drawing signals a breakthrough in terms of Jeanneret's architectural interests and development. He goes beyond surface, skin, and ornamental detail to look at

Painting of *The Ascension of St. John* by Giotto at Santa Croce, Florence, 1907, pencil and watercolor on paper, 18.5 x 20.3 cm. FLC 2263

space and construction details. The drawing includes a representational, perspectival painting of interior space (upper-left-hand corner) and then breaks down the space into one-point perspectives and elevations. The drawing of the roof truss (lower-right-hand corner) is an analysis of structure and architectural assembly and an inquiry into the process of construction.

Court of the Bargello, Florence, October 1907, pencil and gouche on paper, 25 x 36 cm. FLC 2494

With construction beginning in 1255, the Bargello, a former barracks and prison turned art museum, is the oldest public building in Florence. The three-story structure includes an open courtyard and an outside staircase. In the center of the courtyard is an open well. Jeanneret's pencil drawing is an analytical study supported by extensive notes that investigates the elevation and its architectural components, including a column capital and window details. The painting is much more spatial: inclusion of the staircase gives it a three-dimensional quality, and the colors of the loggia lend depth.

Court of the Bargello, Florence, October 1907, pencil, ink, and watercolor on paper, 21.3 x 22 cm.
FLC 5867

Santa Maria del Fiore and Palazzo Vecchio, Florence, 1907, pencil and watercolor on paper, 13.7 x 17.7 cm. FLC 1979

The painting of Santa Maria del Fiore and Palazzo Vecchio harks back to Jeanneret's earlier studies of landscape and topography (such as his study of the Jura landscape on page 50). The abstract, formal notions of the dome are related to the rolling hills beyond through color and form. This sketch suggests cityscape as landscape, a theme he pursued in his travels to Vienna and Paris.

Done in grayscale, the simple study of an architectural detail (opposite) is on a larger piece of paper than Jeanneret typically used. Here he investigates the form of a capital through light, shadow, and value. These two paintings illustrate Jeanneret's ability to zoom in and out. In contrast to some of the more intense drawings from this trip, he used very little line work here.

Study of capital and cornice, pencil and watercolor on paper pasted on cardboard, 32.5 x 25.3 cm. FLC 2178

ABOVE: Interior of the cathedral, Siena, October 5, 1907, pencil and watercolor on paper pasted on cardboard, 21 x 20.6 cm. FLC 2465 OPPOSITE: Palazzo Grottanelli, Siena, 1907, pen and watercolor on paper, 24.8 x 11.3 cm. FLC 2125

On September 29, Jeanneret and Léon Perrin left Florence for a five-day trip to Siena. As the following pages show, Jeanneret produced a wide range of work there, impressionistic drawings as well as analytical sketches. He was interested in both the micro and the macro, studying interior spaces, facade details, urban plans, and building massings. Within each drawing he demonstrated a keen ability to focus even further—to capture, catalog, and convey only certain aspects of what he saw.

The view of the second floor of the Palazzo Grottanelli is, remarkably, from a vantage point where one cannot actually stand. It appears as though Jeanneret had levitated twenty feet into the air, given how accurate the painting is. He does not draw everything: the drawing loses and gains detail as he depicts brick in certain places and not others, allowing the viewer's eye to fill in what is missing. While during this trip he let most of the watercolor washes dry before applying a second wash, here he seems to apply washes more quickly, wet on wet, causing the colors to bleed into each other.

The interior perspective of the Siena cathedral captures a variety of elements: highly detailed surfaces, interior space and light, all working together to evoke a strong sense of atmosphere and life. This drawing is powerful. While the painterly quality is the same as in the sketch of the Palazzo Grottanelli, the perspective is different. The painting of the palazzo is about surface, with no real light source; the interior drawing embodies place and space.

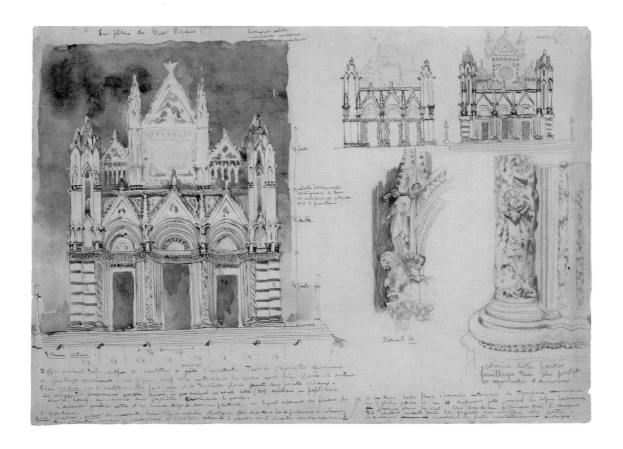

Cathedral facade and details, Siena, 1907, pencil, ink, and watercolor on paper, 25.5 x 34.5 cm. FLC 6055

Jeanneret's intense studies of the two-dimensional aspects of architecture are clearly depicted in his drawings of the two main elevations of the Cathedral of Siena. The watercolor and pencil sketches above are of the main entrance to the Cathedral, which is located in the center of the Piazza del Duomo and appears as a singular facade within the urban square. The second watercolor and accompanying pencil sketches (on the facing page) are of the Baptistery, located at the opposite end of the Cathedral's main entrance, at a slightly lower elevation and rooted within the fabric of the city. He was careful to depict these conditions in each drawing, though his primary goal was to analyze the

facades. By sketching both elevations in quick pencil vignettes, he is able to understand the proportions and rhythms of each facade: how each breaks down in terms of structural bays and punched openings. The vignettes also enable him to organize the larger drawing on each sheet. Below each of the larger drawings is the preestablished proportional system he set up as a guide. He then portrayed the details, the pattern work of mosaics, and how the color and architecture work together. The materiality of the building is reinforced by his limited, two-toned sepia palette, though in the second drawing he added touches of pink watercolor to depict the actual marble.

Baptistery facade and details, Siena, 1907, pencil, ink, and watercolor on paper, 21 x 20.6 cm. FLC 1791

Palazzo Pubblico, Siena, with the Torre del Mangia, 1907, pencil and watercolor on paper, 18.5 x 16 cm. FLC 2852

These drawings capture place, atmosphere, and experience at a specific moment in time as opposed to straightforward documentation of a building. They were done, as historian H. Allen Brooks has noted, after a passing thunderstorm that left an extraordinarily wide range of color and light on the square. We can speculate that the sketches' wet, loose quality is due to Jeanneret's haste in capturing the moment.

After the storm, Church of San Domenico, Siena, October 1907, pen and watercolor on paper, 14.8 x 10.3 cm. FLC 1917

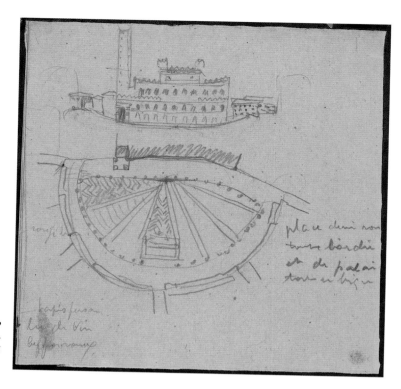

Piazza del Campo, Siena, pencil on paper, 14 x 14.3 cm. FLC 2115

Clearly the defined urban space of the Campo in Siena made an impression on Jeanneret. Up to this point, he had been making drawings and paintings primarily in perspective and had yet to draw a floor plan of a building or a site plan of an urban space. His sketch of the Piazza del Campo is purely architectural: orthographic studies in the form of a site plan and an elevation. This drawing foreshadows the development of the visual note-taking methods that would appear in Germany and his Journey to the East.

On October 7, Jeanneret headed west for an overnight stay in Lucca. As in his earlier studies of the cathedral in Pisa (page 65), here he is studying the rhythms of the bays as well as surface treatment of pattern and materials. Done in grayscale, this drawing is a more painterly exploration of facade: what the details look like takes precedence over dissecting and analyzing the components.

San Martino, Lucca, October 1907, pencil and watercolor on paper, 25.6 x 21.3 cm. FLC 2464

San Vitale, Ravenna, October 1907, pencil, ink, and watercolor on paper, 20 x 19 cm. FLC 1970

Doge's Palace, Venice, 1907, pencil and ink on paper, 24.8 x 32 cm. FLC 2176

These two images, like Jeanneret's decorative drawings of the floor patterns of the Baptistery in Florence and the tabernacle detail at Orsanmichele, explore pattern and ornament, color, and geometry in a highly detailed and expressive architectural form: the details are drawn in perspective, emphasizing the three-dimensionality of pattern and ornament.

The painting of the column capital decorated in richly colored Byzantine marble carvings/mosaics in the Church of San Vitale was made during a six-day stay in Ravenna, one of several stops Jeanneret made en route to Venice after Lucca.

In the sketch of Doge's Palace, which he made in Venice during the final two weeks of his Italy tour, Jeanneret contemplates the joining of ornament and structure, as he figures out how the stone works to support the quatrefoil detail.

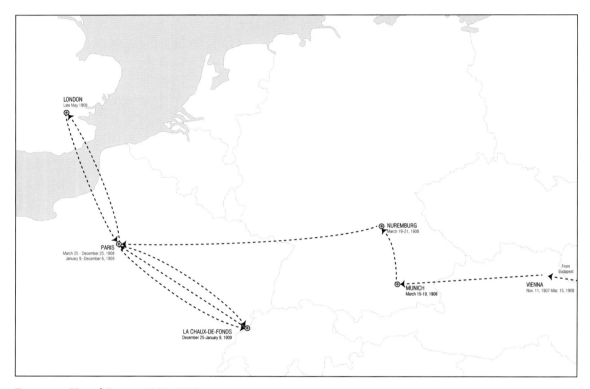

LONDON
Late May 1909

PARIS
March 25 - December 25, 1908
January 9 - December 6, 1909

NUREMBURG
March 19-21, 1908

MUNICH
March 15-19, 1908

VIENNA
Nov. 11, 1907-Mar. 15, 1908

From
Budapest

LA CHAUX-DE-FONDS
December 25-January 9, 1909

European Travel Route: 1907–1909

Europe

Concluding the traditional drawing tour of Italy, Jeanneret, with his friend Léon Perrin, took off to explore more of Europe. Jeanneret was still unsure whether he wanted to be an artist, and he began for the first time to contemplate architecture as a profession. Their first stop was Vienna, where they stayed from November 1907 to March 1908 and Jeanneret completed his first architectural design work—for two villas back home in La Chaux-de-Fonds. Stopping briefly in Nuremberg, Germany, to draw, they then set off for Paris seeking architecture apprenticeships. Bringing with him his drawing sketches of Italy, Jeanneret convinced architect Auguste Perret of his drawing abilities and was hired to work in the Perret Brothers' office. Though Perrin returned home in July 1908, Jeanneret remained in Paris for twenty-one months—until December 1909—while he began searching for a theoretical position to frame his thoughts and future work. He read voraciously, worked with math tutors, and spent time in libraries reading history. In Paris he was also introduced to the new structural technology of reinforced concrete, which forced one to rationalize structure (although his drawings never explored these new concepts). He returned home at the end of 1909 for a few months.

While they were not drawing "tours," Jeanneret's short-term stints away from home are integral to understanding his theoretical development and expanding visual exploration. The drawings he made in Europe during this time serve as the transition between his early watercolor paintings and the visual note taking that would dominate in later travels.

The subject matter he chose to draw was fairly random, given his vacillating interests in art and architecture. For instance, he spent significant time in museums drawing historical room installations, furniture, and artifacts, and he also spent time drawing people. He continued to draw elaborate architectural patterns, corner details, and the profiles of cathedrals that were typical of his earlier, colorful studies in Italy. However, now a city dweller, he started to notice the skyline and medieval streetscapes—the urban context, looking at the city as a larger composition made up of an ensemble of buildings and streets, rather than individual buildings and objects. With a better understanding of the relationship of architecture, landscape and topography, he explored how the contours of the land merged with the forms of buildings in one conversation. This shift in focus from the details of single buildings to the composition and arrangement of an urban ensemble would form the basis for his life-long investigations in city planning.

Jeanneret's watercolor technique also evolved and became much more "painterly." In general, he moved away from time-intensive, detailed, and precise drawings towards quicker, looser studies. He applied fewer washes, used more water, and appears to have painted wet-on-wet. He also limited his palette and left paintings unfinished in places, perhaps to allow for clarity and ambiguity at the same time. These "unfinished" and ephemeral drawings allow the viewer to fill in the unrendered parts. This gap between the realistic elements and the abstract nature of the drawing offered Jeanneret a new point of departure. In drawing things more abstractly, he gave himself room to make creative interpretations on his ever-expanding subject matter, a skill that would eventually translate into his own designs.

Because Jeanneret was not following a specific travel itinerary during this period, the chronology of the drawings is less important, and they are grouped here to illustrate particular points about his use of media, technique, and subject matter.

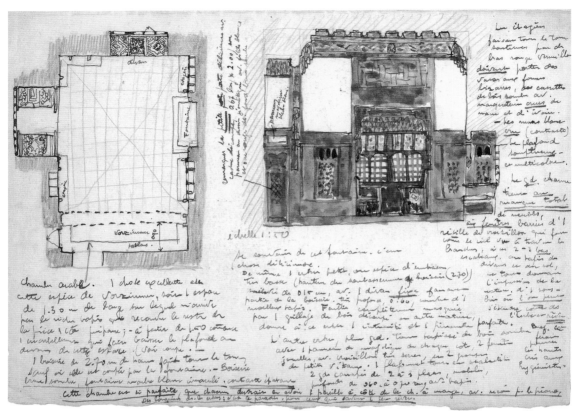

Plan and section of an Arabian Room in the Museum of Decorative Arts, Vienna, pencil, ink, and watercolor on paper, 24.5 x 33.5 cm. FLC 2082

Jeanneret arrived in Vienna on November 11, 1907. He made very few drawings during his four-month stay, perhaps because he was working on the designs for two houses (Stotzer and Jaquemet villas) under L'Epplatenier while he was there. As Allen Brooks has noted, he also indicated in letters to L'Epplatenier that he was unmoved by Vienna's architectural scene, in particular the avant-garde architecture of Otto Wagner and Josef Hoffman, whose work championed the rational clean lines and new materials of the machine age over ornament and detail. With little interest in the built environment here, he spent much of his free time in museums making drawings.

Three drawings are of a museum installation of an Arabian Room. The first is telling in Jeanneret's architectural development. Rather than painting a picturesque, detailed perspective, here he first begins to explore conventional architectural representation—drawing an actual plan and section of the interior using traditional architectural drawing methods, understanding space through the room's floor plan and cross section. This kind of architectural representation demands an understanding of how materials form the profile and the edge of a room. Inherently spatial, plans and sections establish interior relationships, distances, and proportion.

The second drawing is a perspective view of the corner profile Jeanneret drew in plan and section in the first drawing. Full of color, it focuses on the elaborate architectural detailing in the Arabian Room and explores the geometric designs used to make the transition from wall to ceiling to wall to door opening.

The third drawing integrates both studies into one sheet. Jeanneret makes a perspective drawing in watercolor of the ceiling, but also includes a more measured, cross-section sketch through the ceiling (made in pencil) to depict the recessed nature of the ceiling's profile. Combined, these drawings form a collection of architectural studies of the space, with plans and sections (orthographic drawings) and perspectives.

An Arabian Room, formerly in the Museum of Decorative Arts, Vienna, pencil, ink, and watercolor on paper, 34 x 24.5 cm. FLC 2081

Perspective details of an Arabian Room, Vienna, pencil, ink, watercolor, and gouache on paper, 34 x 24.4 cm. FLC 2055

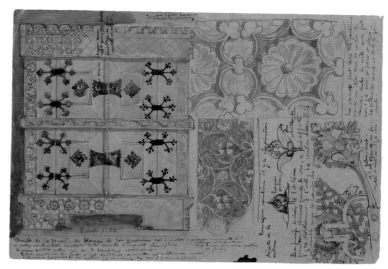

Gothic chest, Österreichische Museum für Kunst und Industrie, Vienna, pencil, ink, and watercolor on paper, 36 x 25 cm. FLC 1989

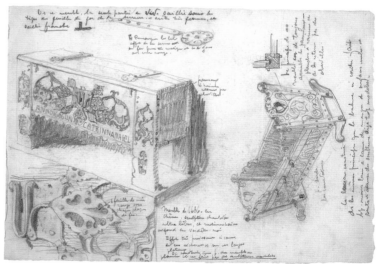

Furniture details, drawn while touring museums, Paris, 1908/09, pencil on paper, 24.3 x 33.8 cm. FLC 1990

In these drawings (the first of which was made in a museum in Vienna and the second two from museums in Paris), one can see Jeanneret's continued interest in surface patterns and the geometries of ornamental details. In the second drawing of furniture details, he makes perspectives, axonometrics, plans, and section details (note the inset sketch of a joint detail, at the top right above the crib), which reveal Jeanneret's developing interests in construction and assembly.

Floral patterns, possibly drawn while touring museums, Paris, 1909, pencil on paper, 49.5 x 32.3 cm. FLC 5849

Portrait, unknown subject, 1909, pencil, watercolor, and gouache on paper, 22.2 x 21.9 cm. FLC 2193

Jeanneret's curiosity led him to draw all sorts of subjects, including people occasionally. This portrait of an unknown subject demonstrates his growing sense of authorship and reflects his evolving and more painterly watercolor technique. That he left the drawing unfinished in places is one reason that it works so well: the unpainted areas make a clear contrast between the portrait and the surrounding context.

Medieval fortifications and watchtowers, Nuremberg, Germany, March 1908, pencil and watercolor on paper, 19.8 x 12.1 cm. FLC 2031

While en route to Paris, Jeanneret stopped briefly in a number of German towns, among them the medieval city of Nuremberg, where he was enthralled by the numerous watchtowers and fortifications of the Middle Ages. These drawings introduce the idea of place in Jeanneret's sketches. They are profoundly urban. They explore the relationship between the medieval buildings and the landscape (how architecture is carved into or built on the topography). Jeanneret highlights the zig-zagging nature of the stairs and the roadways as they work themselves

Medieval fortifications and watchtowers, Nuremberg, Germany, March 1908, pencil and watercolor on paper, 28.2 x 20.7 cm. FLC 2088

Medieval fortifications and watchtowers, Nuremberg, Germany, March 1908, pencil and watercolor on paper, 19.8 x 12 cm. FLC 2099

up through the hills, and he acknowledges the tower as both a visual marker and a tool to define urban space. These first exercises of drawing medieval cities provide the visual groundwork for the position he would later take in his book *Urbanism* (1925), where he celebrates the winding road over the grid. Though compositionally Jeanneret directs his cone of vision up towards the tower, the drawings are primarily about the circulation between the architecture and the earth and the interplay of weight, mass, and gravity.

Paris rooftops, with Notre-Dame in the distance, 1908, pencil and watercolor on paper, 20.5 x 25.5 cm. FLC 1921 R

Once in Paris, Jeanneret made some drawings right from his room in Quai St.-Michele, overlooking Notre-Dame Cathedral. From 9 rue des Écoles, he painted beautiful cityscapes that suggest he began to see the city as he once saw the Jura landscape. Like his landscape paintings, these drawings are expansive, use distant horizon lines, and suggest a sense of looking "out" into the vista as opposed to looking "at" a specific object. They capture the spatial organization of forms and roofs over a collective field rather than capturing one building. In some, instead of drawing only the cathedral, he used its distant spire to punctuate the landscape of Paris.

Technically, these drawings mimic the loose, aqueous style of his drawings in Nuremberg, done in the same size on similar paper and likewise built out of quick pencil sketches. There are at most five layers of watercolor washes.

Skyline of Paris, with Notre-Dame in the distance, painted from Jeanneret's room at 9 rue des Écoles, July 1908, pencil and watercolor on paper, 36 x 25.2 cm. FLC 1924

Paris rooftops, with Notre-Dame in the distance, 1908, watercolor on paper, 25 x 18 cm.
FLC 1920

Notre-Dame, Paris, 1908, pencil and watercolor on paper, 24.2 x 17.3 cm. FLC 1923

Here Jeanneret made two drawings on one sheet of paper—one of Notre-Dame and the other of the nearly complete Sacré-Coeur. While Jeanneret's watercolor technique was becoming less time intensive and less precise, these two watercolors are exceptions: they took more time, were more carefully constructed, and relied on a more controlled application of water. He is again drawing from an elevated position, seeing the city from above, but he focuses more on how major civic pieces of architecture rest in the city. In the drawing of Notre-Dame, he edits the roofscape in the foreground to highlight the spire. Using an intense application of paint, he exaggerates the bell towers, the center steeple, and—notably—includes all the residential chimneys in the foreground.

In the second drawing he omits many of the small buildings of the cityscape leading up to Sacré-Coeur by blurring and simplifying the middle ground. This heightens the monumental role and placement of the church at the top of a hill in the distance. In both cases, the editing out of smaller details gives the drawing a point of view and conveys a message about the lessons Jeanneret is trying to take away.

Notre-Dame and Sacré-Coeur, Paris, 1908/09, pencil, watercolor, and gouache, 28.9 x 22.5 cm.
FLC 2195

Spire details, Notre-Dame, Paris, 1908/09, pencil on paper, 32.5 x 25.2 cm. FLC 2177

In addition to making drawings on loose sheets of paper, Jeanneret filled an entire sketchbook with Notre-Dame (it is still unpublished and in a private collection), concentrating on decoration as opposed to the building's role within the city. Though the two sketches here are loose drawings (one of Notre-Dame focusing on the silhouette of the spire and on its details and another of a cathedral steeple in Chartres), they exemplify Jeanneret's growing ability to zoom in and out.

114

Steeple, Chartres Cathedral, Chartres, France, 1908/09, pencil on paper, 36 x 28.5 cm. FLC 1925

Versailles, France, 1908/09, ink and watercolor on paper, 31 x 40 cm. FLC 2180

In May 1909 Jeanneret's parents joined him in Paris, and together they visited Versailles for the first time. Shortly after his parents' visit he returned to make a number of drawings of the space. The assembly of sketches above, which were quickly built, are some of the first of his sketches ever presented as small vignettes—that is, they were not used to set up larger drawings. These little line drawings capture the sense of place, the pictorial and expansive open space of Versailles, the formal edges of the garden and landscaping, and the many thresholds and gateways designed into the landscape, and they are illustrated using penciled floor plans, notes, eye-level perspectives, and aerial views. The following representational drawing captures the palace complex as a "scape" as he has done with the city skyline and the Jura landscapes. He also takes time to zoom in on the details of the garden, as shown

Versailles, France, 1908/09, pencil, ink, and watercolor on paper, 27.8 x 36.3 cm. FLC 4061

Garden, 1909, pencil, watercolor, and gouache on paper, 20.7 x 28.3 cm. FLC 2192

in the third drawing, of a reflecting pool. The drawing is an unusual composition with the horizon line almost at the top of the page. One can see Jeanneret's layered painting process at work here, with the most detailed and clearly defined area at the top of the page. He leaves the lower part of the drawing unfinished, though he includes a lightly penciled perspective drawing of the overall garden.

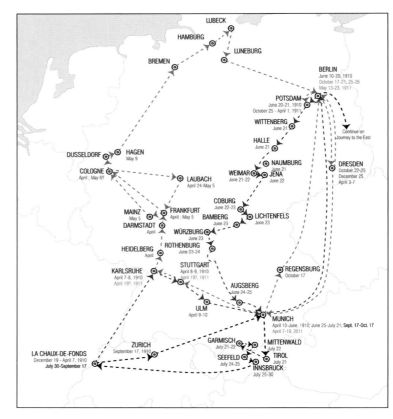

Germany Travel Route: 1910 – 1911

Germany

After Paris, Jeanneret returned home for several months to visit with L'Epplatenier before taking off for a thirteen-and-a-half-month stay in Germany. The first seven months of his trip were dedicated to two research projects that L'Epplatenier had created and helped fund for his former student: analysis of Germany's urban centers and a study of the impact of schools teaching decorative arts on local industry. This analysis was to be used in two separate works—a book Jeanneret and L'Epplatenier would coauthor, *La Construction des Villes*, and a report entitled "Étude sur le Mouvement d'Art Decoratif en Allemagne."

In the five months that followed (November 1910–April 1911), Jeanneret worked as an apprentice at the office of architect Peter Behrens in Berlin. Jeanneret had met August Klipstein several months before, and together they had planned a trip to the East. Though Jeanneret had intended to work at Behrens's office longer, he decided to cut his time short and spent the remaining month in Germany traveling with Klipstein.

To complete his work for L'Epplatenier, Jeanneret traveled around Germany, visiting decorative-arts schools in Weimar, Hamburg, and Düsseldorf. He walked the central core of many small medieval towns and garden cities (such as Stuttgart, Ulm, Wittenberg, Halle, and Naumburg) and visited the major cities of Munich, Potsdam, and Berlin (including Berlin's newly built suburbs of Nikolassee, Zehlendorf, and Neubabelsberg). He also headed off the beaten path into the mountains to draw in Mittenwald and Innsbruck.

Given his extensive itinerary in the first few months, Jeanneret had to cover a lot of ground rather quickly and as a result began to develop a new, shorthand method of visual note taking. Most of the time he spent actually writing about the places he saw as opposed to drawing them, although he would occasionally supplement the text with quick sketches—plans, elevations, small urban diagrams, streetscapes. Jeanneret noted the orientation, main public spaces, and public and private institutions (programming) that anchored the urban centers. He studied how the larger, more iconic buildings defined public space; how they created, or broke free from, the urban edge of the inner square; and how they posed as part of the city fabric.

While writing, he also began to collect—and draw on the back of—travel postcards, and he turned to sketchbooks as his primary recording device. In Germany he completed approximately six sketchbooks, or "carnets," as he called them. As noted earlier, the contents (including notes) of four of the carnets can be found in Giuliano Gresleri's *Les Voyages d'Allemagne: Carnets*. A fifth sketchbook, from his travels in Germany and the East, is reproduced in Gresleri's *Voyage d'Orient: Carnets*. (The sixth carnet, named by Gresleri the "Green Carnet" for the color of its cover, remains unpublished.)

Amid his notes on city centers and the practices of decorative-arts schools, Jeanneret took the time to do some quick studies in the carnets; when he had longer periods to sit and paint, he worked on loose sheets of paper. On the following pages are examples of both.

Jeanneret left La Chaux-de-Fonds for Munich, making one-day stops along the way. These sketches of urban intersections in the towns of Stuttgart and Halle are drawn on the back of postcards, which offered a quick way of capturing the place visually.

Postcard of Geiss-Strasse, Stuttgart, April 1910. La Chaux-de-Fonds Library

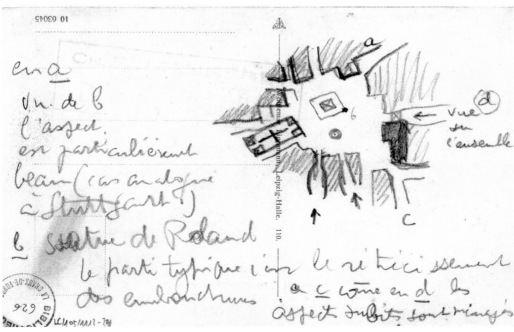

Postcard of Halle, June 1910. La Chaux-de-Fonds Library

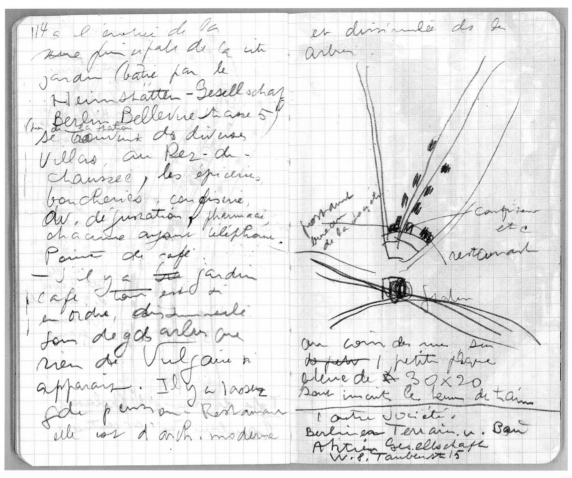

Notes, 1910, pencil, *Les Voyages d'Allemagne*, Carnet 2, pp. 114–15.

Two examples from Carnet 2 typify the style of drawing and the media that Jeanneret relied on during his
sojourn in Germany. Notes and sketches are made in a
pocket-sized notebook with thin, lined paper ideal for
note taking. All four pages focus on urban planning.
The first two pages include notes and a quick sketch of
where two train lines converge in Berlin-Nikolassee; the

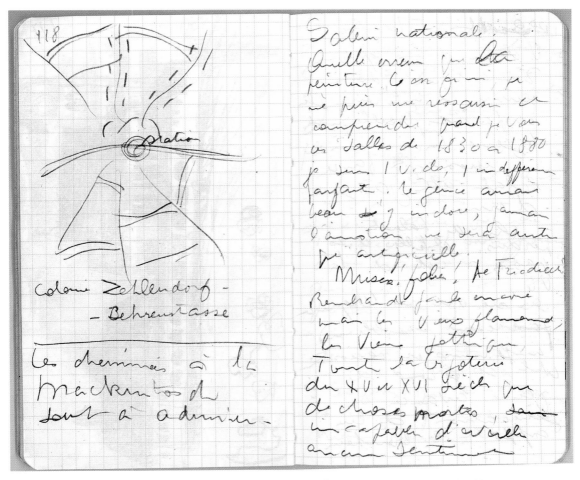

Sketch of Nikolassee Station, 1910, pencil, *Les Voyages d'Allemagne*, Carnet 2, pp. 118–19.

second spread includes notes and a sketch of the plan of Nikolassee Station, the intersection of Behrenstrasse and the Wannsee Bahn.

These sketches, and the watercolors on the next four pages were made during Jeanneret's first trip to Berlin and its surrounding suburbs, a ten-day trip June 10–20, 1910.

Nikolassee Station, 1910, pencil and watercolor, *Les Voyages d'Allemagne*, Carnet 2, pp. 116–17.

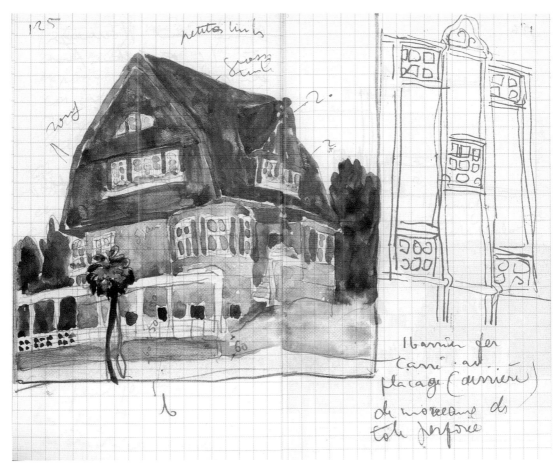

House, 1910, pencil and watercolor, *Les Voyages d'Allemagne*, Carnet 2, pp. 125–26.

Four colorful quick watercolor studies made in the sketchbooks include one with two elevations of Nikolassee Station. The pencil version was likely done first: not only is it not scaled to the page correctly, it is purely about the building and does not include the large tree in the foreground, the plinth on which the building sits, the forest in the distance, or the horizon. The watercolor, on the other hand, includes the ingredients that interested

Courtyard housing, 1910, pencil and watercolor, *Les Voyages d'Allemagne*, Carnet 2, pp. 32–33.

Jeanneret at this time—the building and its relationship to the urban landscape. It is compositionally divided into two horizontal halves and possesses more depth, with landscape and context.

These three watercolors of housing (places unknown) were also done very quickly. Both the pencil line work

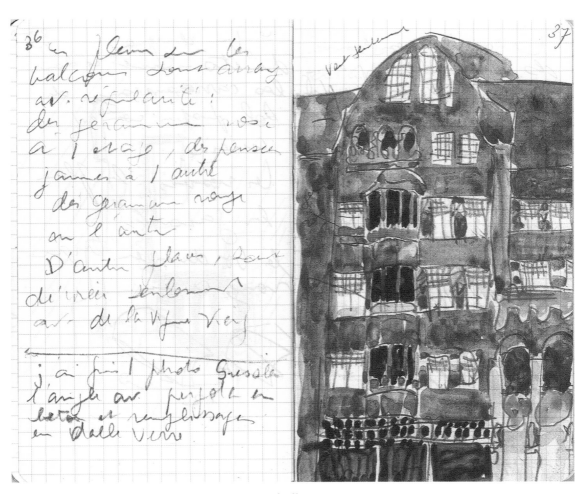

House, 1910, pencil and watercolor, *Les Voyages d'Allemagne*, Carnet 2, p. 37.

and the application of paint are very loose, and the fearless use of color is almost to the detriment of the drawings. The first drawing also shows another new drawing technique: Jeanneret noted the colors of the building and the landscape in pencil, which suggests that he might make a quick pencil sketch and apply the paint later.

Peterskirche, Munich, 1910–1911, pencil and watercolor on paper, 20 x 28.2 cm.
FLC 2041

These watercolors and those that follow from the period were done on loose sheets of paper rather than within the carnets: Jeanneret was giving himself time enough to make slightly longer drawings. While he was mainly interested in urbanism because of his projects with L'Epplatenier, he did study single buildings from time to time. In the drawing of the tower of Peterskirche, he was presumably interested in form—a very complex amalgamation of geometries, including the joining of an octagonal and rectilinear apse, a cylindrical stair tower, and pyramidal roofs.

The chapel and the rural outbuilding on the following page, drawn while Jeanneret was hiking through the Tirol mountains with his former classmate Octave Matthey, are seen as objects but, unlike the study of the Peterskirche, here the context is not completely eliminated.

Chapel Mittenwald, Germany, July 24, 1910, pencil and watercolor on paper, 27.5 x 20 cm.
FLC 1759

Rural outbuilding, Innsbruck, Germany, July 25, 1910, pencil, watercolor, and gouache on paper, 26.5 x 19.2 cm. FLC 2199

Nymphenburg Palace, Munich, 1910–1911, pencil and watercolor on paper,
17.4 x 24.8 cm. FLC 2053

Jeanneret's investigations of architecture and urbanism during this period of time
fueled a shifting attitude towards classicism. As Brooks has noted, "In April 1910,
Jeanneret arrived [in Germany] a medievalist, in May 1911 he departed a classi-
cist." The two images of palace complexes, above and overleaf, reflect this new-
found interest.

The eighteenth-century Nymphenburg Palace, which features a restrained,
cubic pavilion and impressive grounds, was among Jeanneret's favorite subjects.
He included the formal court in front of the palace, clearly recognizing the important relationship between the architecture and the open space that precedes it.

The drawing of the Sanssouci palace was made on an afternoon trip to Potsdam.
Designed and built between 1745 and 1747, the palace, a smaller and rococo German
counterpart to Versailles, served as the summer home of Frederick the Great. Jeanneret understood the axial and symmetrical nature of the terraced gardens, as he
drew the grand stair and approach, rendering the natural, reflective quality of water
and the formal geometries of the trees as they define a highly controlled landscape.

Orangerie at Schloss Sanssouci, Potsdam, 1910, pencil and watercolor on paper pasted to cardboard, 29.2 x 22 cm. FLC 2857

Frauenkirche, Munich, Germany, 1910–1911, pencil, watercolor and ink on paper. Institut für Geschichte und Theorie der Architektur ETH Zurich

Three drawings embody Jeanneret's interests in urbanism. In the drawing of the twin towers of Frauenkirche (above), he pays particular attention to form and silhouette, eliminating all surface detail on the facade of the church and delineating only the two large bell-tower openings to emphasize the cathedral's mass, profile, and iconic nature within the city fabric.

The drawing of Frankfurt (overleaf) was made shortly

Frankfurt, April 1911, pencil and watercolor on paper, 40.5 x 40.5 cm. FLC 2855

Odeonsplatz, Munich, 1910–1911, pencil on paper, 12.6 x 20 cm. FLC 2030

after Jeanneret left Behrens's office. Interested in the city's many layers and how they work together to create a composition, he captured in loose detail the everyday fabric of the city, the infrastructure of the bridge, the river, and the iconic tower that punctuates the skyline.

The view toward Odeonsplatz in Munich is one of Jeanneret's longer studies, given the extensive pencil work. Drawn in one-point perspective, the sketch is primarily a streetscape: pedestrians on the sidewalk and the city streets leading into the main public square. Secondarily, the drawing investigates the placement of buildings fronting the square.

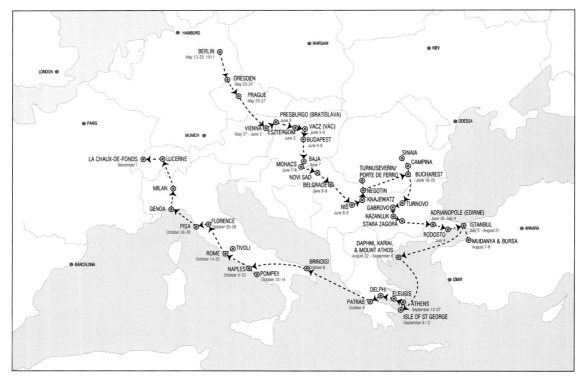

The East Travel Route: 1911

Journey to the East

On May 23, 1911, Jeanneret set out with Baedeker in hand and, along with travel companion August Klipstein, left for southeastern Europe. Starting in Berlin, they headed to Vienna and then worked their way through the Balkans, Turkey, and farther south and west to Greece, at which point Klipstein returned home. Jeanneret then traveled alone to southern Italy via Naples, Pompeii, Rome, Pisa, and Milan, before returning to Switzerland.

By this time, Jeanneret had begun to synthesize what he had learned over the past ten years. He studied ruins and notable buildings and zoomed out to draw the city's culture and urban spaces as if he were seeing it all from an airplane. In trying to discover something new, he also looked beyond the monuments to the everyday (much as the German architect Karl Friedrich Schinkel did during his grand tour at the beginning of the nineteenth century). He drew peasants' houses, people, simple pots, food, and furniture, and made urban diagrams; he revisited his earlier childhood interests from La Chaux-de-Fonds such as plants, animals, and geometric floor patterns. Now, however, he saw these as part of the city and culture, and as an expression of cultural aesthetics rather than as objects in and of themselves. He drew panoramas and skylines, making note of where the architecture ended and the sky began. In doing so, he recognized that the line—made by and informed by nature and man together—creates a moment of architectural emotion. He also began to see that nature's geometries were the same universal shapes that were applied to art, architecture, and urban form. This broadened perspective and understanding of the inherent consistencies within the structural development of the natural and built environments would become the philosophical underpinning of his design education. The process of drawing was the vehicle that helped him to see and then to understand and refine his world view.

Jeanneret's means of note taking included photography, drawing, painting, and writing. The camera took the place of picture postcards, though sketchbooks remained his primary recording device. During this trip, he made all sorts of drawings—representational, abstract, and analytical. The fast, shorthand method he developed in Germany became more prevalent: many of the drawings almost look like earlier work: he was interested now in the idea above all else. He drew diagrammatic, severely edited plans, sections, and perspectives and pure forms (domes, spheres, cones, cylinders) to get at the essence of the place. He also engaged other drawing conventions, such as axonometrics, bird's-eye and fish-eye views, to capture expansive and intimate spaces respectively.

Most of the drawings were done in pen and pencil and highlighted with colored pencil, but he also continued using watercolor, sometimes experimenting with new techniques that resembled those of other artists of the time, such as a series of highly stylized paintings of Istanbul's harbor life (Sailboats in the Sea of Marmara (pages 164 and 165). These impressionistic paintings, along with a similarly stylized pen-and-ink drawing of the House in Bulgaria (page 148) include short, bold brush or pen strokes that suggest texture and movement. In addition to his sketches and paintings, he wrote prolifically—to L'Epplatenier, his parents, and friends, and he made extensive entries in his sketchbooks. The clarity and insight of his written observations matched the clarity of his drawings, and he became as skilled a writer as he was an artist. (For a collection of his writings, see *Journey to the East,* edited by Ivan Zaknic.)

Knize Gentleman's Outfitters on the Graben (Adolf Loos, architect), Vienna, June 1, 1911, pencil and color pencil, *Voyage d'Orient*, Carnet 1, p. 57.

Der Goldene Pelikan, Jeanneret's hotel in Vienna, 1911, pencil and colored pencil on paper, 20 x 25.3 cm. FLC 1910

Jeanneret and Klipstein arrived in Vienna on May 27, 1911, and stayed for six days. Jeanneret mostly sketched furniture and interior decor there, but he also began to explore everyday buildings such as the exterior of a retail shop (designed, ironically, by Adolf Loos, who was arguing for architecture without exterior ornament) and the courtyard of his hotel. Both drawings were quickly drafted, with small touches of color.

The route from Vienna to Turnovo was quite an adventure. As Brooks outlined in *Le Corbusier's Formative Years,* the two young men took a steamer down the Danube River towards Budapest, then traveled by boat to Belgrade, making a brief stop in Baja to hunt for pots. (Jeanneret had become particularly interested in pots and other folk art after meeting William Ritter in Germany.) From Belgrade they hiked into the Serbian highlands towards Bucharest, finally arriving by rail at the ancient capital of Turnovo.

Built into steep cliffs above the Yantra River, this stunning city is famous for its architecture. The old city (known as the City of the Tsars), atop three hills, features palaces, churches, and civic architecture attributed to Bulgaria's Second Empire. Enraptured, Jeanneret made a number of drawings of the city from different locations and documented it in photographs.

In this sketch of Turnovo, Jeanneret used a bird's-eye, or aerial, view, an ideal convention for illustrating the urban form of the city and its relationship to topography and the natural world. To create depth of field, he adds more detail to the right side of the drawing and then, as the city curves back into the landscape, the pencil work gradually becomes more gestural, with less detail and more emphasis on larger elements of landscape and horizon, a drawing technique that echoes his earlier landscapes (see, for example, pages 46 and 48).

View of Turnovo, Bulgaria, June 1911, pencil on paper, 12.7 x 20 cm. FLC 2496

The drawing of a church in the town of Gabrovo (just southeast of Turnovo) relies on the loose and sketchy watercolor technique that Jeanneret used in Germany. His focus is on the relationship of public space and iconic architecture from the viewpoint of the pedestrian.

Church in Gabrovo, Bulgaria, June 1911, pencil and watercolor on paper, 31 x 40 cm. FLC 2853

Jeanneret and Klipstein took the Shipka Pass, a rough and rocky but scenic mountain pass through the Balkan Mountains, to get from Gabrovo to Kazanlak. He made an extremely powerful drawing, captioned "On the route to Kazanlak, 27 June," en route. Utterly transporting, it makes you feel as if you are right there with him in the back of the horse-drawn cart. You can feel the immediacy of the experience as he might have felt it. The

Sur la route de Kasanlic 27 juin

Cart driver and horse,
pencil on paper, 20 x
12.5 cm. FLC 2498

expanse of his creative search is also evident: here is one of his own intimate interactions with people, the everyday social and cultural experiences of his travels. The drawing demonstrates a mature draftsmanship and facility in delineating only the lines that matter. The pencil work is swift and confident. There is no fussing to find the right line, and he needed only very few lines to capture the overall experience.

Here we can see Jeanneret's continued exploration of vernacular architecture and the deployment of a more stylized drawing technique using pen as his primary medium. The textural strokes are reminiscent of Van Gogh's drawings of rural farmland and give equal life and emphasis to architectural and landscape elements.

House in Bulgaria, June 1911, pencil, ink and colored pencil on paper, 29 x 39 cm. FLC 1793

Caravansary of Erdine, 1911, pencil on paper, 17.2 x 23.7 cm. FLC 6107

Jeanneret's first stop in Turkey was the ancient capital of Erdine, in the northeast part of the country just over the border of Bulgaria. During his short stay he drew and photographed the famous mosques but, again, turned to the everyday architecture of the place as well, as shown in this drawing of an inn with a central courtyard. Exploring the subject from an architectural point of view, he analyzes the main idea—the courtyard—and the flow of space. On the right side of the sheet is a quick sketch of the interior plan of the courtyard and the spatial sequence from street to interior. The larger, one-point perspective from the street into the courtyard is framed by the inn's symmetrical, vertical circulation. Here, Jeanneret seems to pry open the entry sequence, drawing it in such a way as to allow the viewer to experience the different sequences of spaces, walking up the stairs or entering the courtyard.

Wooden house, Constantinople (Istanbul), July–August 1911, pencil and watercolor on paper, 11.3 x 19.4 cm. FLC 6111

After Erdine, the young men sailed off toward Constantinople, where they stayed seven weeks, taking up residence in a room overlooking the Golden Horn, the estuary that feeds into the Bosphorus strait and the Sea of Marmara. Literally horn-shaped, the estuary creates a peninsula, the tip of which is where the ancient part of the city lies, separated from the rest of town. Jeanneret made many drawings, from panoramic views to detailed drawings of vernacular houses both rural and urban. The larger sketch (above) is from a vantage point that looks downhill and includes hints of red and blue watercolor wash that highlight the building's wood cladding and upper columns. The smaller pencil drawing in the upper corner looks uphill at the same building. The notations concern the proportions of the facade as well as its rhythm and bay structure.

Courtyard house, Eyup, 1911, pencil and watercolor on paper, 12.5 x 20.0 cm. FLC 1792

Three drawings (above and following pages) explore the architecture of the courtyard house at different scales: the building's exterior and its relationship to the street and adjacent buildings, its interior courtyard spaces, and architectural details.

Courtyard house, pencil, ink, and watercolor, 21.3 x 16.3 cm. FLC 2046

Entry/door detail, pencil and watercolor, 25.5 x 18 cm. FLC 2035

While Jeanneret was in Istambul, he was absorbing the city from different vantage points, capturing skylines that define both the southern and northern borders of the city. It is noteworthy that he was deploying multiple techniques to convey different ideas about what are essentially similar skyline views.

The very atmospheric panoramic drawing of Istanbul looks south toward Constantinople from his room, highlighting the silhouettes of the mosques against the sea beyond. In the foreground, subtly, he paints a bridge with piers, and he uses a range of light-to-dark values to capture the Golden Horn that separates Pera from the old city.

In contrast, the profile of Pera (page 156) documents the northern skyline through a more architectural lens. Made much more quickly and with less finesse, this diagram is a study of form and profile. (Note: the yellow square is the residue from a piece of tape stuck to the drawing.)

Panorama of Istanbul, Sea of Marmara in the distance, July 1911, pencil and watercolor on paper, 9 x 30 cm. FLC 1794

The view of the Bosphorus (page 156) was made looking back at Constantinople from a boat and is yet another example of how Jeanneret looked at similar subjects by means of different media.

The view from Taksim (page 157) zooms out, capturing both edges of the city simultaneously, with Pera in the foreground and Constantinople in the distance. The two versions on the sheet are very loose but powerful studies representing the same cityscape. With very few (and wet) strokes, Jeanneret makes only the most essential notations to describe the view and heighten its sense of mystery.

Notably, the drawings of Istambul (above), Pera, and Taksim were made on loose sheets of paper, while the fourth sketch was made in his carnet (according to Brooks, this drawing was made during Jeanneret's departure from Constantinople, while his ship to Mount Athos was quarantined for several hours).

Profile of Pera (Istanbul) with Galata tower, July 1911, pencil on paper, 11.5 x 18.2 cm. FLC 6113

View of Bosphorus, Istanbul, 1911, pencil, *Voyage d'Orient*, Carnet 3, p. 37.

View from Taksim, Istanbul, 1911, watercolor on paper, 40.5 x 31.3 cm. FLC 1938

Café of Mahmoud Pacha, Istanbul, 1911, pencil on paper, 13 x 19.3 cm. FLC 1880

Jeanneret explores the interior courtyard of a cafe as its own world, separated from the street, using a fish-eye view (an enclosed perspective) to capture an enclosed space.

He employs the more traditional architectural convention, the axonometric, to decode and understand the integration and symbiosis of overall building forms and

Aerial axonometric view of Hagia Sophia, Istanbul, 1911, pencil on paper, 12 x 16.5 cm. FLC 6073

space. This view of the Hagia Sophia campus not only helps the viewer to understand the layout of the site and the elements within it (towers, bridges, courtyards) but also reveals mass, volume, and scale. This approach also demonstrates how a building's floor plans are integral to and inseparable from its elevations and roofscape, as both are represented simultaneously in the drawing.

Yesil Turbe (Green Tomb), Bursa, Turkey, 1911, pencil and watercolor, *Voyage d'Orient*, Carnet 3, p. 15.

Yesil Mosque (Green Mosque), Bursa, Turkey, 1911, pencil, *Voyage d'Orient*, Carnet 3, p. 28

During his stay in Istanbul, Jeanneret ventured south by sea for a two-day trip to Bursa, Turkey. There he made numerous drawings in his carnet, including six pages of drawings of the Yesil complex alone. The Green Tomb, the mausoleum for the fifth Ottoman sultan, Mehmed I, is a hexagonal, domed building perched on top of a hill above the rest of the complex. Jeanneret's drawing of it is built of a quick pencil sketch with a few washes of watercolor to signify the vibrance of the exterior green tiles. Quite painterly, it captures the structure's picturesque nature.

The Yesil Mosque, one of the earliest examples of Ottoman architecture that originated in Bursa in the fourteenth and fifteenth centuries, merged volumetric Byzantine structures such as the Hagia Sophia with highly decorative, arabesque traditions. Jeanneret drew the mosque's vast inner spaces created by the introduction of vaults and domes in the transverse sectional drawing (above) and delineated its space and circulation in a plan that also noted a doorway detail (opposite).

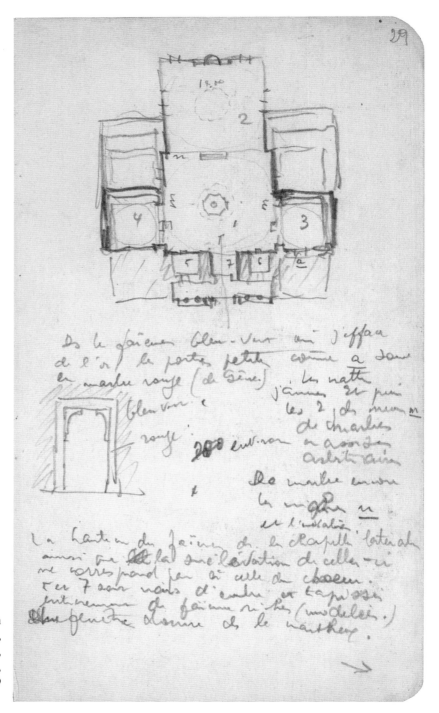

Yesil Mosque (Green
Mosque), Bursa,
Turkey, 1911, pencil,
Voyage d'Orient,
Carnet 3, p. 29

Northwest facade of Suleymaniye Mosque, Istanbul, 1911, pencil on paper, 12.5 x 20.2 cm. FLC 2384

Jeanneret continued to study Ottoman imperial mosques, such as the monumental structure of the Suleymaniye Mosque, which is the largest mosque in Istanbul. In this drawing he explores the pedestrian approach as well as the building's mass, volume, and scale.

Sailboats in the Sea of Marmara, with Constantinople in the background, pencil, ink, and watercolor on paper, 25.2 x 32 cm. FLC 2858

Sailboats in the Sea of Marmara, with Constantinople in the background, pencil, ink, and watercolor on paper, 23.2 x 29 cm. FLC 1939

Jeanneret is seeing the world through the eyes of an artist in these drawings of the cultural and social life on the Sea of Marmara. Like his drawing of the peasant house in Bulgaria on page 148, these are very stylized, illustrative paintings reminiscent of other painters in terms of composition and technique. The drawing is gestural and dynamic, capturing the sailboats, waves, and clouds all in motion.

The Acropolis, Athens, September 1911, pencil on paper, *Voyage d'Orient*, Carnet 3, p. 123.

From Istanbul to Athens was a grueling three-week trip for Jeanneret and Klipstein: Jeanneret was sick during his stay on Mount Athos (a remote, mountainous peninsula in the Aegean Sea, occupied entirely by monks), and the ship was quarantined because of a cholera scare, postponing their arrival until the morning of September 12, 1911. Jeanneret waited until the late afternoon, just before sunset, before heading to the Acropolis. He would stay in Greece for a total of three weeks and would draw the Acropolis and the Parthenon many times and from different vantage points. These drawings convey his exhaustive visual examination of the site as he moved around, making drawings and paintings from afar and close up, from below looking up, both outside and inside it, and looking out from inside. So moved by the perfection of this one site, it was here that Jeanneret stated he would become an architect.

The Acropolis, Athens, pencil on paper, 27 x 21.4 cm. FLC 2454

This reductive drawing speaks to form: the natural rock formation of the Acropolis and the man-made Parthenon have been fused together and drawn as one integrated, monolithic mass.

Plan and elevation of the Propylaea, Athens, 1911, pencil, *Voyage d'Orient*,
Carnet 3, pp. 106–07.

Here Jeanneret organizes the plan of the approach up to the
Parthenon and includes a perspective view of the Propylaea.
These two drawings, made one right after the other, help one
to appreciate how a two-dimensional orthographic plan will
actually be experienced in three dimensions. This kind of study
is an invaluable drawing exercise for understanding space.

Columns of the Parthenon,
Athens, September 1911,
pencil and watercolor on
paper, 21.2 x 13.2 cm. FLC
1782

As in so many of Jeanneret's vista sketches, the fast
watercolor drawing of the columns of the Parthenon
studies the relationship between architecture, landscape,
sea, and sky, here with an emphasis on verticality.

Columns of the Propylaea, Athens, September 1911, pencil and watercolor on paper pasted on cardboard, 17 x 26.3 cm. FLC 2849

These two drawings again emphasize and celebrate the relationship between the man-made (the carved stone columns of the buildings) and the natural world (the Mediterranean Sea and sky beyond). Long vertical brush strokes express the fluting of the columns. The paint runs right up to the edge of the paper: each is on a small sheet of loose paper mounted onto a larger

Columns of the Parthenon, Athens, September 1911, pencil and watercolor on paper, 13.3 x 21.7 cm. FLC 2850

piece of cardboard that presumably lends a more rigid surface upon which to draw. The cardboard also provides a strong framing device that mimics a camera view finder. Unlike the expansive views Jeanneret made in Istanbul, these drawings are not about the panoramic view; they are very controlled, "framed" compositions.

Temple of Jupiter (with its reconstruction sketched below), Pompeii, 1911, pencil, 28.6 x 24.7 cm. FLC 1937

The Forum, Pompeii, 1911, pencil and watercolor on paper, 23.5 x 32 cm. FLC 2859

August Klipstein headed home on September 27, leaving Jeanneret to complete the remainder of his tour alone. He arrived in Italy on October 6. Stopping briefly in Naples, he made his way to Pompeii for a five-day drawing expedition. The perspective drawing of the temple of Jupiter includes Mount Vesuvius in the background as a contextual and orienting device; the image below is a looser, quicker drawing of the same perspective, drawn with the original form and context reconstructed. By reimagining the temple, he took documentational drawing into the design world. In the watercolor drawing, he repositions himself inside the temple to sketch the view looking out into the space and "completes" the now broken columns in order to envision the original view.

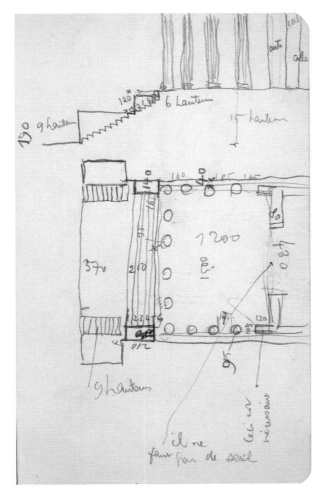

Plan and section, Temple of Jupiter, Pompeii, pencil, *Voyage d'Orient*, Carnet 4, p. 105.

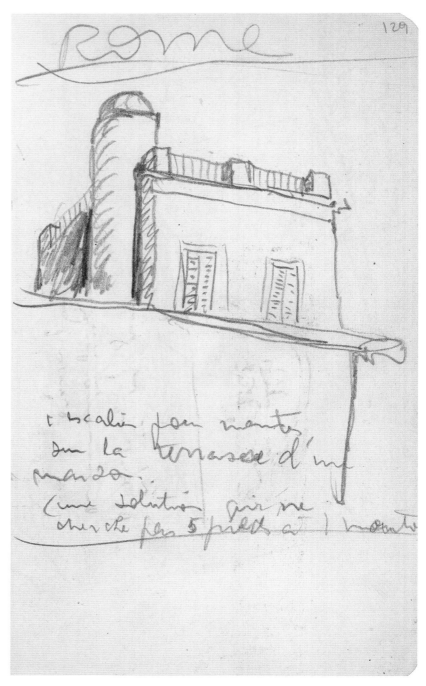

Rome, 1911, pencil, *Voyage d'Orient*, Carnet 4, p. 129.

Rome, 1911, pencil and colored pencil, *Voyage d'Orient*, Carnet 4, pp. 134–35.

Jeanneret arrived in Rome on October 14, 1911, boldly making note of his new location in his sketchbook (opposite, his drawing of a subject unknown). It was his first visit, and he studied many of the city's major architectural monuments. In the two drawings of St. Peter's Basilica and the Vatican walls (above) he tested different techniques to compare the effect of value obtained through shades of light and dark with line work. The top drawing (which presumably preceded the lower) is made predominantly of lines or "edges," especially evidenced in his depiction of the urban fabric in the foreground. In the second drawing, Jeanneret again pressed sharply on the pencil but only to draw the profile and the windows. He adjusted his technique to illustrate the urban fabric, giving it greater dimension and depth of field through shaded values, here by turning the pencil on its side and rubbing the lead to create the buildings in the foreground.

Basilica di Maxentius, Rome, 1911, pencil, *Voyage d'Orient*, Carnet 4, p. 138.

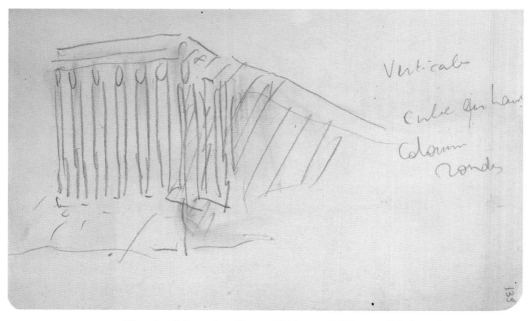

Temple of Antonius, Rome, 1911, pencil, *Voyage d'Orient*, Carnet 4, p. 139.

Pyramid of Caius Cestius and Hadrian's tomb, Rome, 1911, pencil, *Voyages d'Orient*, Carnet 4, p. 141.

While we see the emergence of Jeanneret's visual note taking in Germany, he really made the most of—and mastered—the technique in Italy. He focused on geometric solids in Rome—domes, spheres, pyramids, and cylinders—all primal three-dimensional shapes from which architecture could be conceived and built. Here he made a number of diagrammatic studies looking at buildings and reducing them to their essential shapes. These studies would help cultivate a life-long curiosity with pure form.

Here, from a side trip to Tivoli (see pages 184–86), Jeanneret's catalog of the geometric solid forms at Hadrian's Villa.

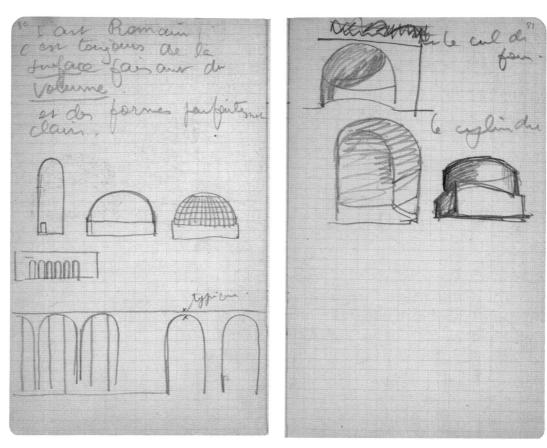

Hadrian's Villa, Tivoli, 1911, pencil, *Voyage d'Orient*, Carnet 5, pp. 80–81.

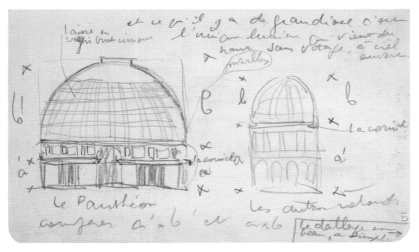

The Pantheon, Rome, 1911, pencil, *Voyage d'Orient*, Carnet 4, p. 151.

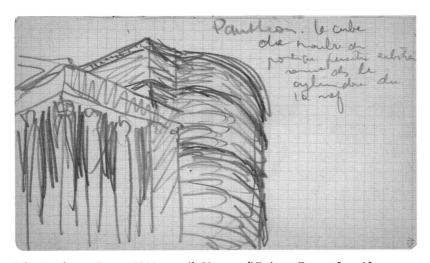

The Pantheon, Rome, 1911, pencil, *Voyage d'Orient*, Carnet 5, p. 13.

Jeanneret made a number of drawings and notes on the Pantheon (although sur-prisingly never a watercolor). In one drawing, he investigates the sectional nature of the space and its proportional system, in comparison to another dome; the other, the exterior viewed from the corner of Via Crescenzi and the Piazza della Rotonda, clearly delineates the moment when the form of the drum and the form of the portico converge.

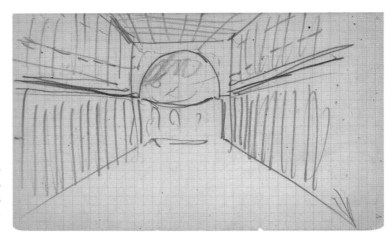

Central nave, Santa Maria Maggiore, Rome, 1911, pencil, *Voyage d'Orient*, Carnet 5, p. 1.

Santa Maria Maggiore, Rome, 1911, pencil, *Voyage d'Orient*, Carnet 5, p. 2.

Santa Maria Maggiore, Rome, 1911, pencil, *Voyage d'Orient*, Carnet 5, p. 3.

Santa Maria in Cosmedin, Rome, 1911, pencil, *Voyage d'Orient*, Carnet 5, p. 9.

On his first trip to Italy in 1907, Jeanneret drew church interiors and was consumed by surface details and frescoes. Now he was understanding space and profile. The three interior drawings of Santa Maria Maggiore are of the central nave: the top pencil sketch is a one-point perspective depicting the box-like shape of the nave and its formal terminus; the middle sketch is a sectional perspective, a convention he used very rarely, but here it best conveys his observations, capturing both the arches and space of the side aisles and the coffered ceiling in the central nave. The last sketch notes the abundant columns that organize the interior.

Jeanneret was also fond of the basilica of Santa Maria in Cosmedin, where he sketched the central nave in perspective and made a second, smaller diagram of the sectional and spatial relationships between the two side aisles and the central nave.

Jeanneret was also studying Rome's urbanism. He made quick diagrams of urban spaces throughout the city: here, the plan of Piazza Navona with the significant architectural anchors of the space: Bernini's three fountains and Borromini's Church of Sant'Agnese; and a plan and perspective sketch of Michelangelo's Campidoglio. (The perspective view below the plan is oriented in the same direction, which allows one to better understand this site's organization.)

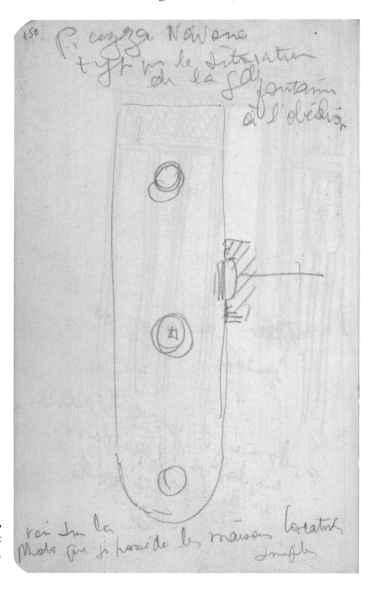

Piazza Navona, Rome, 1911, pencil, *Voyage d'Orient*, Carnet 4, p. 150.

Campidoglio, Rome, 1911, pencil, *Voyage d'Orient*, Carnet 4, pp. 176–77.

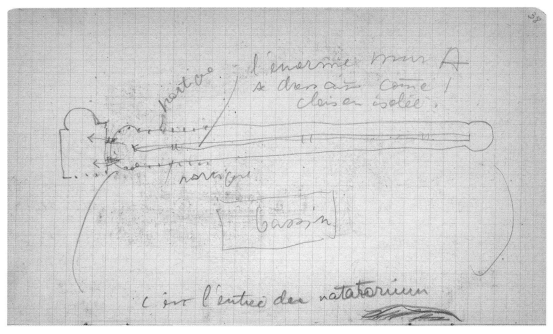

Hadrian's Villa, Tivoli, 1911, pencil, *Voyage d'Orient*, Carnet 5, p. 38.

Jeanneret spent only two weeks in Italy, mostly in Rome, but did venture to Tivoli to visit Hadrian's Villa as well as Villa d'Este, making this stop the last major visual exploration of his Journey to the East. Most of Carnet 5 is filled with notes and sketches of the complex at Hadrian's Villa. He documents how the wall of the villa helps to organize the sprawling terrain and terminates with an apse where the topography drops off; he also studies, though perspective and sectional sketches, the primal form of the dome that encloses the baths.

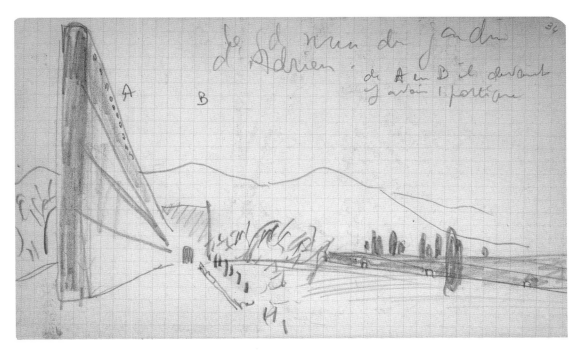

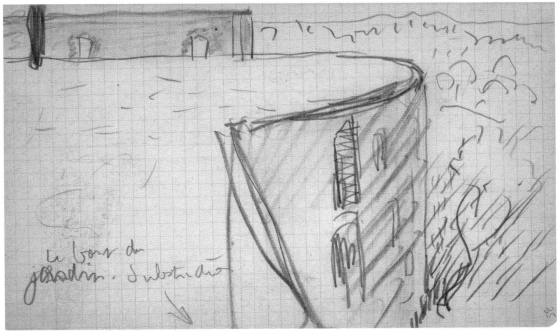

Hadrian's Villa, Tivoli, 1911, pencil, *Voyage d'Orient*, Carnet 5, pp. 34–35.

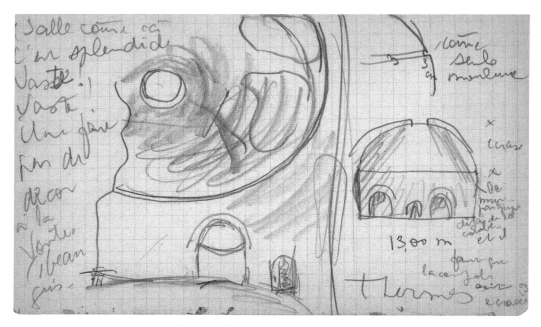

Baths at Hadrian's Villa, Tivoli, 1911, pencil, *Voyage d'Orient*, Carnet 5, p. 63.

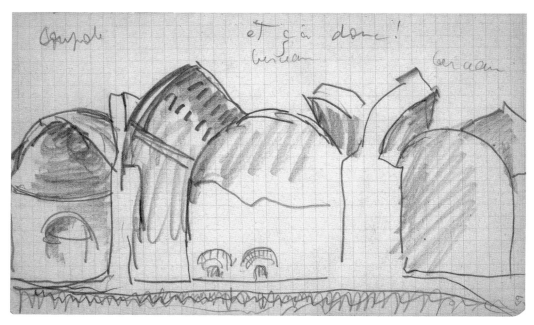

Baths at Hadrian's Villa, Tivoli, 1911, pencil, *Voyage d'Orient*, Carnet 5, p. 65.

Baptistery, Pisa, 1911, pencil on paper. FLC 2491

Jeanneret's seven-month journey was coming to an end. He headed north toward Switzerland, passing through Florence and Pisa again, taking time to redraw Pisa's cathedral complex four years later. If we compare this drawing to his earlier studies of Pisa on pages 65 and 67, we can see that Jeanneret is looking back at the same site with new eyes, now recognizing the urban design principles that organize the individual buildings. Whereas before he had drawn facade and surface details of each structure independently, he now sees how the buildings relate to one another and function as definers of space: he recognizes that the Baptistery is on axis with the main cathedral and sets up the terminus of the complex. He also captures the composition and pure forms of the buildings. The cathedral on the left and the Campo Santo on the right are planar forms that set off the more sculptural aspect of the Baptistery's dome. We can also see how his technique has evolved. This drawing is a quick pencil sketch made with a blunt pencil in contrast to earlier drawings that rely on extensive and precise line work.

Columns of the Parthenon, Athens, September 1911, pencil and watercolor on paper, 21 x 13.7 cm. FLC 2851

Conclusion

Jeanneret was a very forward thinker. From a young age, he was in pursuit of a set of principles that would guide him in a creative profession for the rest of his life. Travel drawing served as his education and his rite of passage. For him, the *process* of drawing was the vehicle that helped him see and then to understand and then to refine and develop his world view.

How does one learn to see in order to know?

The first step in learning to see is to learn to draw. To learn to draw, you need to make representational drawings of what you see.

This level of engagement forces you to really *look at* and study the subject. Most people think they understand what they are looking at, but in reality do not really see the individual details, the shapes and components that make up an object or a scene. Through real-time reflection, the act of drawing is inherently self-informing and self-instructive, as it requires you to analytically decode a building, landscape, or the nature of place. You have to visually take the building apart, door by door, and put it back together on paper. As soon as you put pencil to paper, you are forced to take account of size, notice sun and shadow, and so on.

The next step in learning to see is drawing the subject at different scales—zooming in on the details and looking at its larger form, capturing it from different perspectives, through different drawing conventions, and with various media. This also requires you to choose and decide—quickly or slowly—what you want to include, leave out, emphasize, rearrange, or even distort. The immediacy of the onslaught of information as well as decisions required on-site are at once overwhelming and exhilarating. This moment of authorship and abstraction ensures new paths for discovery and simultaneously presents infinite avenues for the drawing to inform you.

It is critical to study different subjects in the same way—not just scenic landscapes or buildings, but people, art, urban space, plants, and so on: the process provides for a much larger and richer visual vocabulary.

With the skills of representational drawing and different drawing conventions mastered, you essentially learn to see. Now you can begin to understand, and to draw, what is behind what you see. You can recognize and draw the idea embedded in the reality, or look behind the curtain to see what makes the subject work. You find the visual principles (form, light, shadow, material, composition, color, proportion) that are built into the timeless aesthetics of art and architecture. Drawing allows the exploration of these malleable principles that are in constant flux, capable of evolution and invention.

The lessons Jeanneret learned during his early drawing expeditions would go on to coalesce in his manifesto in *Vers une architecture*, perhaps the most influential architecture book of the twentieth century.

Whether you are Jeanneret working in the swells of the industrial revolution or a global architect working with cutting-edge computer software programs in the twenty-first century, or simply interested in the creative search, there will always be immeasurable value in making travel drawings. In the authentic and active experience of drawing—of physically recording what we see—we bring back with us a new way of seeing; we bring back sketchbooks full of information, analysis, and an understanding of cultures, histories, and places, the emotion, memories, sounds, and smells of new and foreign places, and all the other elements that make what we see matter.

References

Baker, Geoffrey H., and Le Corbusier. *Le Corbusier, the Creative Search: The Formative Years of Charles-Edouard Jeanneret.* New York: Van Nostrand Reinhold, 1996.

Brooks, H. Allen. *Le Corbusier's Formative Years: Charles-Edouard Jeanneret at La Chaux-de-Fonds.* Chicago: University of Chicago Press, 1997.

Le Corbusier and Giuliano Gresleri. *Les Voyages d'Allemagne: Carnets.* Milan: Electa, 2002.

———. *Voyage d'Orient: Carnets.* Milan: Electa, 1987.

Le Corbusier and Ivan Žaknić. *Journey to the East.* Cambridge, Mass: MIT Press, 1987.

Le Corbusier, Stanislaus von Moos, and Arthur Rüegg. *Le Corbusier Before Le Corbusier: Applied Arts, Architecture, Painting, Photography, 1907–1922.* New Haven: Yale University Press, 2002.